Wallace Stegner's Salt Lake City

Wallace Stegner's

SALT LAKE CITY

Robert C. Steensma

THE UNIVERSITY OF UTAH PRESS
Salt Lake City

The Defiance House Man colophon is a registered trademark of the
University of Utah Press. It is based upon a four-foot-tall, Ancient
Puebloan pictograph (late PIII) near Glen Canyon, Utah.

11 10 09 08   2 3 4 5

LIBRARY OF CONGRESS CATALOGING-IN-PUBLICATION DATA
Steensma, Robert C., 1930-
   Wallace Stegner's Salt Lake City / by Robert C. Steensma.
      p. cm.
   Includes bibliographical references.
   ISBN 978-0-87480-898-8 (cloth : alk. paper) 1. Stegner, Wallace Earle, 1909-1993—Homes and
haunts—Utah—Salt Lake City. 2. Stegner, Wallace Earle, 1909-1993—Homes and haunts—West (U.S.)
3. Authors, American—Homes and haunts—Utah—Salt Lake City. 4. Authors, American—20th
century—Biography. 5. West (U.S.)—Intellectual life—20th century. 6. Utah—Intellectual life—20th
century. 7. West (U.S.)—In literature. 8. Utah—In literature. 9. West (U.S.) —Biography. 10. Utah—
Biography. I. Title.
   PS3537.T316Z463 2007
   813'.52—dc22
   [B]   2007018935

To the memory of

Brendan Thompson (1996–2002)

beloved grandson

Contents

Acknowledgments   *ix*

PART I   Salt Lake City   1

Crossroads of the West   3

Salt Lake City   19

East High School   33

The University of Utah   43

PART II   Wallace Stegner on Salt Lake City   59

"At Home in the Fields of the Lord" by Wallace Stegner   61

"It Is the Love of Books I Owe Them" by Wallace Stegner   71

PART III   Photo Essay   79

PART IV   Maps   153

Notes   159

Bibliography   163

Acknowledgments

I N THE FALL OF 1955, when I was an untested young instructor of English at Augustana College in Sioux Falls, South Dakota, the first novel I taught in my career was Wallace Stegner's first novel, *Remembering Laughter,* which was embedded in our freshman English reader. My enthusiasm for the book was heightened by the fact that my department head, Dr. Don Fryxell, had been a student of Stegner at the "other" Augustana in Rock Island, Illinois.

Late in my career I taught an individual author's course on Stegner for eight years at the University of Utah. Fittingly enough, my last class period before retirement in 2001 was the Stegner class, and my last university lecture was on Stegner's last novel, *Crossing to Safety.* And it was in a Stegner class eight years earlier that a student brought me a news story from the *Salt Lake Tribune* telling of Stegner's eventually fatal injuries in Santa Fe the day before. Thus, in a way, my academic career was framed by Stegner's first and last novels, which led me to write this book.

Many people have made this book a pleasant task. First of all, my editor, Peter DeLafosse, with his encouragement and insights, has proved once again the truth of that old adage that a writer's best friend is a superb editor. Jinni Fontana of the University of Utah Press designed the book beautifully. Dan Johnson and Chevron provided funding for the photographs. And two friends whose parents were close to Stegner during their years at the University of Utah provided photographs, leads, and insights that made my research easier. Anne Riordan gave me information about, and photos of, her mother, Juanita Crawford Broberg (the Nola of *Recapitulation*), and Helen "Peg" Foster (the Holly of the same book). Bob Irvine, the California novelist of the Mormon Manti mysteries, gave me several photographs of his father, Jack Irvine, who is the Joe Mulder of *Recapitulation,* and provided information about Stegner and his university friends.

The staffs at the Utah Historical Society and the J. Willard Marriott Library at the University of Utah were most helpful in helping me find suitable photographs. Dr. Gregory Thompson, Walter Jones, and Madelyn Garrett in the Marriott's Special Collections made things much easier. Dr. Arthur Huseboe and Dr. Harry Thompson of the Center for Western Studies at Augustana College in Sioux Falls were gracious in granting me opportunities to test ideas on them.

For the help I received from others I have not space enough to indicate their specific contributions, but I am deeply grateful to them: Maryan Egan-Baker (for unraveling a genealogical mystery), Jackson Benson, the late Everett Cooley, Glenda Cotter, Vern Gorzitze, John Herbert, Sarah Hoffman, Mike Homer, JoAnn Milner, Richard Milner, Paul Mogren, David Moore, Bill Mulder, James Nelson, Forrest G. Robinson, Page Stegner, Sam Weller, Annette Wenda, the Utah Westerners, the University of Utah Emeritus Club, and the students in my Stegner classes at the University of Utah.

And finally I must thank my wife, Sharon, our children, and some friends who endured my countless stories about Stegner and my guided tours of Salt Lake sites associated with him.

PART I

✦ *Salt Lake City* ✦

Crossroads of the West

OR MORE THAN A CENTURY AND A HALF, Salt Lake City has been unique among American cities religiously, environmentally, and culturally. Founded in 1847, when Brigham Young, second president of the Church of Jesus Christ of Latter-day Saints, or LDS Church, led the main company of 148 people out of Emigration Canyon on July 24 (an advance party had preceded them by two days), the small settlement grew within seven or eight months to 2,200 people, to 6,000 in 1850, and to 77,000 in 1900.

The city in the shadows of the towering Wasatch Mountains soon grew to be not only a haven for a religious group fleeing persecution in Illinois but also the main business center, the Crossroads of the West, between Denver and San Francisco, the headquarters of one of the world's fastest-growing religious denominations and a major cultural, scientific, technological, and educational center of the American West.[1]

Wilford Woodruff, fourth president of the LDS Church, upon his entrance into the valley with Brigham Young, described the landscape in his diary as "a vast rich fertile valley…with the heaviest garb of green vegitation [*sic*]…abounding with the best fresh water springs rivulets creeks Brooks & rivers." Thomas Bullock, a member of the advance party, wrote in his journal for July 22 that the wheatgrass was six feet high and the other grasses ten to twelve. The valley soon became a haven for thousands of people from the eastern and middle western United States as well as northern Europe, particularly Great Britain and Scandinavia, perhaps in response to Bullock's clarion call of 1848: "Come ye poor afflicted people, come and live; come and worship the Lord God of Israel, and let your years be many on the earth."[2]

The pioneers soon began building their city by following the city plan that Joseph Smith (founder of the church), Sidney Rigdon, and Frederick G. Williams promulgated in 1833. Because this was the first and probably most successful urban planning in American history, it is worth quoting at length from B. H. Roberts's history of the church's first century:

> The city plat is one mile square, divided into blocks containing ten acres each—forty rods square—except the middle range of blocks running north and south; they will be forty by sixty rods, containing fifteen acres, having their greatest extent east and west. The streets will be eight rods wide, intersecting each other at right angles. The center tier of blocks forty by sixty rods will be reserved for public buildings, temples, tabernacles, school houses, etc.
>
> All the other blocks will be divided into half-acre lots, a four-rod front to every lot, and extending back twenty rods. In one block the lots will run from the north and south, and in the next one from east and west, and so on alternately throughout the city, except in that range of blocks reserved for public buildings. By this arrangement no street will be built on entirely through the street; but on one block the houses will stand on one street, and on the next one on another street. All the houses are to be built of brick or stone; and but one house on a lot, which is to stand twenty-five feet back from the street, the space in front being for lawns, ornamental trees, shrubbery, flowers according to the taste of the owners; the rest of the lot will be for gardens, etc.

It is supposed that such a plat when built up will contain fifteen or twenty thousand population, and that they will require twenty-four buildings to supply them with houses for public worship and schools. These buildings will be temples, none of which will be less than eighty-seven feet by sixty-one, and two stories high, each story to be fourteen feet, making the building twenty-eight feet to the square.

Further provisions were made for barns, stables, and farms to the north and south of the city, but the farmers were to live in the city to "enjoy all the advantages of schools, public lectures, and other meetings."[3]

The first survey of the city, made by Orson Pratt, assisted by Henry G. Sherwood, on August 31, 1847, located the center at 4327.27 feet above sea level; at latitude 40 degrees, 46 minutes, and 4 seconds; and at longitude 111 degrees, 54 minutes, and no seconds. A plaque sponsored by the Mutual Improvement Associations of the Church of Jesus Christ of Latter-day Saints and the Utah Pioneer Trails and Landmarks Association marks the center of the city on the southeast wall of the Temple Square at Main Street and South Temple. The corner of Main and South Temple became the starting point for the east-west and north-south street-numbering system.

But the human history of Salt Lake Valley began long before 1847. Various American Indian civilizations had lived there as early as 10,000 BC, followed by the Anasazi, Fremont, Ute, Paiute, Goshute, and Shoshoni. Europeans made their first appearance in Utah in 1765, when Juan Maria Antonio Rivera led an expedition that reached areas around present-day Monticello and Moab. In 1776 two Catholic priests, Francisco Atanasio Domínguez and Francisco Silvestre Vélez de Escalante, moved north from Santa Fe with a party of twelve Spaniards and three Ute Indians to find a route to Monterey, California. They entered what is now Utah in late September and reached Utah Valley (the site of Provo) but did not cross the Traverse

Range north of Utah Lake to explore the region of the large lake about which the Indians told them.

It remained for Jim Bridger, the legendary mountain man, to discover the Great Salt Lake in the autumn of 1824, when he floated out of the Bear River on the north side of the lake. Etienne Provost may have seen it a short time earlier. In the decades that followed before 1847, numerous trappers, explorers, and adventurers passed through the valley. John C. Frémont, the famous "Pathfinder," for example, spent time in the area on his exploratory expeditions of 1843 and 1845 (he also came in 1853). Other explorers in the valley included Captain Howard Stansbury, who mapped the Great Basin; Joseph Walker; and Captain Benjamin Bonneville.

And with the explorers came the first travelers to places beyond the valley. The first was the Bidwell-Bartleson party of 1841 on their way to California, and within a few years some migrating groups crossed the valley and the desert to the west. Of these the best known was the tragic Donner-Reed party of 1846 that came through in late 1846 and went on to the horrors of starvation, death, and cannibalism when they were trapped by early snows in the Sierra Nevada on the California-Nevada border. They entered the Salt Lake Valley through Emigration Canyon, which the Mormon pioneers were to use a few years later.

But all those who entered, settled, or passed through the valley were struck by the beauty of the Wasatch, Oquirrh, and Traverse ranges, with peaks towering to more than eleven thousand feet, with the heat and aridity of the summers and the snows of the winters that were later to give the area a reputation for some of the finest skiing in the world. The climate of the valley was and remains fairly temperate when compared with that of the Great Plains, the Midwest, and the East. January high and low temperatures generally fall in the midthirties and low twenties, whereas in July they run in the nineties and midsixties, relieved by low humidity in the teens and cooling canyon breezes at dusk and dawn. One of the later immigrants was to find after years of living from coast to coast that Salt Lake City was his hometown, which he was able to use in several major pieces of fiction and a number of essays.

When George Stegner moved his wife, Hilda, and their two sons, Cecil and Wallace, from Great Falls in the summer of 1921, Salt Lake City was a much larger place than anywhere the family had lived before. It was a growing city that in 1900 was home to 53,531 citizens, but by 1920, the year before the Stegners' arrival, it had grown to 118,110, and by 1940, three years after Wallace Stegner left his teaching position at the University of Utah, its population was 149,934. In the 2000 census, it numbered 181,266, but many of the places that were villages, communities, or small towns in Stegner's time grew rapidly in the late twentieth century: Murray, Midvale, Sandy, South Jordan, West Jordan, Draper, and areas since incorporated such as West Valley City, Holladay, and Cottonwood Heights. When the Stegners were living in Salt Lake City, the city's business district was largely confined to an area between Main and State Streets on the east and west and South Temple and Broadway on the north and south. Centered around the spiritual center of Temple Square, the city was anchored by the state capitol to the north and the University of Utah to the east. Areas such as Federal Heights and those above Foothill Drive were relatively undeveloped, and the southern edge of Salt Lake City itself did not extend much beyond Sugar House. The population of Salt Lake County is now over 1 million.

Salt Lake City was the first place that the Stegners were able to put down any kind of roots, fragile as they might have been. It was a city less than eighty years old, but the completion of the transcontinental railroad on May 10, 1869, at Promontory Summit about seventy miles north-northwest and the completion of the Lincoln Highway through Utah in the 1920s made the city the Crossroads of the West.

Only a quarter century after statehood in 1896, Utah had a population of 449,396 in 1920, just before the Stegners arrived, and was to grow to 507,847 in

1930, when Wallace Stegner graduated from the University of Utah, and to 550,310 in 1940. Utah's population is now more than 2.5 million. To the Stegners, Salt Lake must have seemed a great and wonderful departure from the near-frontier ambience of Saskatchewan and Great Falls. As Stegner was later to describe it in "Finding the Place: A Migrant Childhood," it was "a city in a valley under the lee of mountains, with a glint of the lake off westward." The city with its wide, clean streets, its imposing architecture of Temple Square, the Hotel Utah, the Newhouse Hotel, the Walker Bank building, and the University of Utah, and its beautiful parks caught the eye of young Wallace, as he recalled in the same essay:

> The Mormons who built it and lived in it had a strong sense of family and community, something the Stegners and the people they had lived among were notably short of. My brother and I found, near the first house we moved into, a municipal playground (pronounced muni-sipple), where he, a good athlete, was welcomed and even I was tolerated. We discovered the Mormon institution known as Mutual, for Mutual Improvement Association, which on Tuesday evenings, in every ward house in Zion, provided everything from Boy Scout meetings and Bible classes to basketball leagues and teenage dances. There may have been a covert proselyting motive in the welcome that the wards extended to strange gentile kids, but there was a lot of plain warmth and goodwill, too. I have never ceased to be grateful for what they gave us when what they gave us mattered a great deal; and though I was never tempted to adopt their beliefs, I could never write about them, when it came to that, except as a friend. Their obsession with their history, too, eventually made me aware of growing up entirely without history, and set me on a trail to find or construct some for myself.[4]

The city in the early twentieth century was already a diverse one. As Linda Sillitoe has shown in her *History of Salt Lake County,* Chinese lived in Plum

Alley, which ran between First and Second South between State and Main. On Beck Street west of the capitol was Swedetown. Japanese Town was on 100 South between West Temple and 300 West, Greek Town on 200 South between 400 and 600 West, while Italians lived near the railroads. There were also Little Syria and Lebanese Town around 300 South and 500 West. And in Murray, separated from Salt Lake City by several miles of farmland, there were Croats, Serbs, Slovenes, Norwegians, Danes, Italians, and Japanese who farmed or worked in the smelters.[5]

In 1921 Salt Lake City, according to the 1921 city directory, had more than 140 cafés and restaurants, 400 grocery stores, 170 rooming houses, 130 hotels, and 26 theaters. In 1937 when Stegner, his wife, Mary, and their young son, Page, left for Wisconsin, the city (again according to the city directory for that year) had three daily newspapers (the *Telegram* and the *Deseret News,* both afternoon, and the *Tribune*), 137 churches of sixteen denominations, fifteen hotels with 2,788 rooms, five hospitals, five golf courses, eleven high schools, ten parochial schools, and public schools with an enrollment of 31,628. The Mormon Tabernacle Choir made its first network radio broadcast on July 15, 1939.

In 1920 a Salt Lake City attorney, Parley P. Christensen (1869–1954), became the first Utahn to be nominated and run for the presidency of the United States. Having moved leftward from the Republican Party, he ran on the ticket of the Farm-Labor Party and received 265,000 votes, 4,000 of them in Utah. He later ran unsuccessfully for the United States Senate from Illinois. In 1931 a Salt Lake barber named M. P. Bales ran for Salt Lake mayor on the Communist ticket and finished fourth, with 15 percent of the vote.

By the late twentieth century the city had become a major American intellectual, cultural, and technological center, with the prestigious and highly ranked University of Utah a national leader in medical and computer research; three world-class performance companies in the Utah Symphony, Ballet West, and Utah Opera; and a large number of leading technological firms.

Young Wallace was very much attracted to athletics, although he was not as much a natural athlete as his brother, Cecil. He took his chances with the automobile traffic outside the old Bonneville baseball park on Ninth South between State and Main to shag batting-practice balls hit over the fence in return for a free bleacher ticket.

The Salt Lake Bees had entered the Pacific Coast League in 1915 under the team ownership of H. W. Lane, but were moved to Hollywood after the 1925 season and did not return to the PCL until 1958. As a youngster Stegner saw some of the greats who went on to star in the major leagues: Tony Lazzeri, who set a minor league record with 60 home runs in one season and later became a member of the New York Yankees' Murderers' Row with Babe Ruth and Lou Gehrig; Willie Kamm; Lefty O'Doul; Duffy Lewis; Fritz Coumbe; and Paul Strand, who hit 43 homers and had 325 hits in 1923.

Stegner recounts his youthful experiences with baseball in "At Home in the Fields of the Lord":

> No heroes ever walked so tall as Willie Kamm and Tony Lazzeri and Lefty O'Doul and Duffy Lewis and Paul Strand and Fritz Coumbe of the old Salt Lake Bees in the Pacific Coast League. The year Tony Lazzeri hit sixty home runs over the short left field fence at Bonneville Park I haunted State Street, outside that fence, and risked death in traffic a hundred times to chase batting-practice balls and get a free seat in the left field bleachers. And when Coumbe, who had pitched (I believe) for the Athletics and played against Babe Ruth (Ruth hit the first ball he threw him over the centerfield fence) came to live in the other half of a duplex from us, and brought other heroes home with him, and gave me a left-handed first base mitt that had belonged to George Sisler, I grew twelve inches overnight.[6]

Throughout some of Stegner's work, both fiction and nonfiction, there are memorable descriptions of Salt Lake City. One might recall the opening of *Recapitulation,* for example, as Bruce Mason returns to the city from San Francisco to bury the last remaining member of this family, his aunt Margaret Webb:

> The highway entering Salt Lake City from the west curves around the southern end of Great Salt Lake past Black Rock and the ratty beaches, swings north away from the smoke of the smelter towns, veers around the dry lake bed where a long time ago the domes of the Saltair Pavilion used to rise like an Arabic exhalation, and straightens out eastward again. Ahead, across the white flats, the city is a mirage, or a mural: metropolitan towers, then houses and channeled streets, and then the mountain wall.[7]

Arriving downtown at the Hotel Utah (now the Joseph Smith Memorial Building), he notices few changes since he left the city forty-five years before:

> The city had spread out a good deal, and he was surprised, after the desert, by the green luxuriance of its trees. But the streets were still a half mile wide, and water still ran in at least some of the gutters. It was really a pleasant town; it looked young and vigorous and clean. Passing the Brigham Young monument, he nodded gravely to the figure with the outstretched hand, and like a native coming home he turned at the light in the middle of the block and pulled into the parking garage that had replaced the old Deseret Gymnasium. That change jolted him a little. The old rattrap gym had held a lot of the boy he used to be.[8]

Later, as he looks down from his hotel room overlooking Main and South Temple, he notices the changes:

Progress had been at work on it. Old buildings had been replaced by newer, taller ones, and something drastic had happened to Main Street. Its sidewalks had been widened well out into the former traffic lanes, and the street narrowed to half its width. The sidewalks thus expanded had been encumbered with planters, fountains, flower urns, and stelae, all made of a substance that looked like granite but probably wasn't. The effect was like the Soviet exhibit at a World's Fair, something created by Heroic Workers. Merely human activities would be diminished on such a street. God pity the adolescent who in his exuberance, talking to his girl, turned around and walked backward. God pity the woman who window-shopped as she walked. Ass over teacup into a fountain or a bed of golardias [*gaillardias*].

On the other hand, it did get flowers and young trees into the downtown concrete. It did demonstrate that community pride, half Mormon and half Chamber of Commerce, that had always made Salt Lake a clean and pleasant town.[9]

There are many such passages in *The Big Rock Candy Mountain* and *Recapitulation,* passages that strike a responsive chord in the reader who has lived in Salt Lake City for any length of time. But his fascination with the city can also be found in the essay "Xanadu by the Salt Flats: Memories of a Pleasure Dome," in which he recalls the famous amusement center built on the Great Salt Lake and opening in June 1893 at which Stegner worked during the summer of 1924 after his junior year at East High School.

As he tells us in "At Home in the Fields of the Lord," Stegner later came to realize the rootlessness of his family in Salt Lake City, as does Bruce in *The Big Rock Candy Mountain:*

Long afterward, Bruce looked back on the life of his family with half-amused wonder at its rootlessness. The people who lived a long time in

one place, cutting down the overgrown lilac hedge and substituting bar-
berry, changing the shape of the lily-pool from square to round, digging
out old bulbs and putting in new, watching their trees grow from saplings
to giants that shaded the house, by contrast seemed to walk a dubious line
between contentment and boredom. What they had must be comfortable,
pleasant, worn smooth by long use; they did not feel the edge of change.[10]

It is Elsa, Bruce's mother, who most feels the pain of not finding permanence. In a passage shortly following the preceding one, Bruce thinks,

> She had wanted to be part of something, an essential atom in a street,
> a town, a state; she would have loved to get herself expressed in all the
> pleasant, secure details of a deeply lived-in house. She was cut out to be a
> wife and mother as few women were. Given half a chance, she would have
> done well at it.... But look, he said, at what she had to work with. Twelve
> houses at least in the first four years in Salt Lake, each house with its taint
> from preceding tenants, each with its own invulnerable atmosphere and
> that spiritual scent that the Chinese call the *feng shui.* Twelve houses in
> four years, in every part of the city. They moved in, circled around like
> a dog preparing to drop its haunches, and moved out again without any
> chance of ever infusing any house with the quality of their own lives.[11]

Because George Stegner was always operating at the limits of the law, and
often outside them with his bootlegging and operation of a speakeasy in the family
living room, the Stegners, like the Masons, moved frequently. From a check of the
Salt Lake City directories between 1922 and 1939, we can identify eleven places
where the Stegners lived, but there is no doubt that the family moved so often that
the people compiling the directories were unable to catch up with them.

In 1922 George H. Stegner is listed as a farmer living at 1191 South 700 East, but is not found in the 1923 and 1924 directories. In 1926 he was found at 26 West 400 South. There is no listing for George and Hilda in 1927 or 1928, but the 1927 directory has Wallace listed as a clerk for I&M Rug and Linoleum and living in "rooms" at 1155 East 200 South, while Cecil ("clerk") is in "rooms" at 903 West 200 South. By 1929 George, Hilda, and Wallace are residing at 1148 East 700 South, but Cecil, now married to Elverna (mistakenly listed as Luverne) and working as an attendant for Continental Oil, is living next door at 1150 East 700 South. The 1930 directory finds George ("mining"), Hilda, and Wallace ("salesman") at 1440 South 1500 East.

Cecil died in 1931 of pneumonia after helping a snow-stalled motorist, but in that year's directory his wife, Elverna, is listed as a telephone operator for the Chamber of Commerce and living at 834 Pierpont Avenue (as she would be listed in 1932). George ("mining"), Hilda, and Wallace ("clerk" at I&M) are again found at 1440 South 1500 East. There are no directory entries for 1932 because George and Hilda had moved to Reno, whereas Wallace was a graduate student at the University of Iowa. There are also no listings for 1933, the year in which Hilda died.

In 1934 George is found at two places, Apartment 507 at 125 South 300 East and Apartment 12 at 621 South Temple. Wallace was still in Iowa, and Cecil's widow has not been listed since 1931. Curiously enough, the 1935 directory, which lists George ("salesman") living in Apartment 28 at 53 South 300 East and Wallace and Mary (married in 1934) at 280 G Street, also lists a Patricia A. Stegner, age forty-three, who died on May 13, 1934. A search of the burial records at the Utah State Historical Society reveals that she was born in 1891 as Patricia Agnes Gallagher and is buried in the Park section of the Salt Lake City Cemetery in plot 33-5-3W, not far from George, Hilda, and Cecil. Her relationship to George Stegner, possibly by marriage, is uncertain.

In 1936 Wallace and Mary are living at 1211 East Princeton and in 1937 in Apartment 4 at 270 South 1200 East. George is not listed in either of these years or in 1938. The 1939 directory merely lists George as having died on June 15, 1939.

In the three novels *The Big Rock Candy Mountain, Recapitulation,* and *Joe Hill,* as well as several short stories and essays, Stegner gives the modern Salt Lake City resident a lively and accurate description of the city in the 1920s and 1930s.

In *Joe Hill* (originally titled *The Preacher and the Slave*) Stegner uses a number of historical figures in addition to the title character, who was executed on November 19, 1915, for the murder of a grocer and his son on Salt Lake City's west side on January 12, 1914. Among those historical figures playing important roles in the novel are Governor William Spry, who turned down Hill's appeals; Elmer O. Leatherwood, the prosecuting attorney (though not named in the story; he later served several terms in the U.S. House of Representatives); Morris L. Ritchie, the trial judge; the defense counsels E. E. McDougall, Frank B. Scott, Soren X. Christiansen, and Judge Orrin Nelson Hilton (later disbarred); Dr. Frank M. McHugh, the Murray physician who treated Hill's gunshot wound and later said that Hill had admitted the murders to him; Vera Hansen and Phoebe Seeley, witnesses; E. J. Miller of the Western Arms and Sporting Goods Company; and Chief Justice D. N. Straup of the Utah Supreme Court.

In *The Big Rock Candy Mountain, Recapitulation,* and the short stories "The Blue-Winged Teal," "Maiden in a Tower," and "The Volunteer," Stegner uses people from his experiences at East High School and the University of Utah for his characters, as we will see in the introductions to those sections, but he gives them fictional names. In many other instances Stegner deftly uses setting to evoke feelings and memories. In the two essays reprinted here, for example, he brings back the memories of his youth in Salt Lake City. In "At Home in the Fields of the Lord," he says,

> Because I believe in the influence of places on personalities, I think it
> somehow important that certain songs we sang as high school or college
> students in the twenties still mean particular and personal things. "I'm

Looking over a Four Leaf Clover" is all tied up with the late-dusk smell of October on Second South and Twelfth East [near the university], and the shine of the arc light on the split street tipping up the Second South hill. "When Day Is Done" has the linseed oil smell of yellow slickers in it, and the feel of the soft corduroy cuffs those slickers had, and the colors of John Held pictures painted on the backs. "Exactly Like You" means the carpet, the mezzanine, the very look and texture and smell, of the Temple Square Hotel.[12]

"It Is the Love of Books I Owe Them," his essay about his student years at the University of Utah, opens with a dream:

I am coming along Thirteenth East on my way to an eight o'clock class. It is a marvelous morning—it is always a marvelous morning, whether the air is hazy with autumn and the oakbrush on the Wasatch has gone bronze and gold, or whether the chestnut trees along the street are coned with blossoms. The early sun slants across lawns and throws three-shadows halfway across the pavement and warms the faces of houses on the other side. Cars pass, people wave, walkers across the street give me greeting— faces that I am glad to see, and that are glad to see me. I am enveloped in universal friendliness.... I turn at the drugstore on Second South and start uphill toward the Park Building at the head of the U drive.[13]

Or he can evoke the memories of Saltair, a pleasure palace on the shores of the Great Salt Lake, where he worked at age fifteen for one summer. Saltair operated from 1893 to its closing in 1958. Stegner remembers the resort, regretting that his grandchildren will never know about his glorious summer:

They do not know what they have missed, but I am sorry for them anyway. They will never know the thrill of working in an enchanted palace whose onion domes float on the desert afternoon, and whose halo of light at night pales the starts. They know not the sound of gritty salt underfoot, or the sight of potted palms glittering with salt like tinsel. The smell of the humble hot dog cooking will never arouse them, as it does me, to uncontrollable glossolalia. Their ears will never prick, as mine do, to the spectral chanting of barkers, the thunder and screams from the roller coaster, the sob of saxophones on the dance floor. Nor will they ever hear, in intervals of quiet, the slap of heavy waves down under, down in the caverns measureless to man among the pilings. I went down there once, wading chin deep, and found the place shadowy, lit by flashes and reflections like a sea cave, and haunted by spiders as big as walnuts.

And he concludes, "Saltair lingers in memories other than mine, a mirage, a fairyland that promises, at least to fifteen year olds of all ages, perpetual glamour."[14]

Salt Lake City was more than just a home for Stegner during the fourteen years he lived there. The city provided him with an education, matured him socially and intellectually, and gave him a rich fund of associations and memories to use in his fiction, his historical writing, and his environmental work.

Salt Lake City

WHEN GEORGE STEGNER brought his wife, Hilda, and their two sons, Cecil and Wallace, to Salt Lake City in the summer of 1921, young Wallace was to find the place he was later to call his hometown. When he went east for graduate work in 1930, he found himself longing for the valley of the Great Salt Lake, as he says in "Finding the Place: A Migrant Childhood":

> I suppose I learned more, and faster, during two years in Iowa City than in another two-year period in my life, and some of what I learned was about myself. I had always known, not entirely happily, *what* I was. I was a target. Now I began to understand *who* I was. I was a westerner.
>
> Homesickness is a great teacher. It taught me, during an endless rainy fall, that I came from arid lands, and liked where I came from. I was used to a dry clarity and sharpness in the air. I was used to horizons that either lifted into jagged ranges or rimmed the geometrical circle of the flat world. I was used to seeing a long way. I was used to earth colors—tan, rusty red, toned white—and the endless green of Iowa offended me. I was used to a sun that came up over mountains and went down behind other mountains. I missed the color and smell of sagebrush, and the sight of bare ground.[1]

"I have always envied people with a hometown," Stegner wrote at the beginning of his famous essay "At Home in the Fields of the Lord." "They always seem to have an attic, and in the attic albums of pictures, spellers used in the third grade, gocarts and Irish mails with the scars of young heels and teeth on them."[2]

During his eighty-four years before his death in 1993, Stegner crossed the United States as a professor, a writer, and an environmentalist. He lived in many places from Massachusetts to California. In his childhood and adolescence he was dragged by his restless father and nest-seeking mother from Iowa to North Dakota to Washington State to Saskatchewan to Montana to Utah. In Salt Lake City the family was constantly on the move because of George's bootlegging. During his professorial career, Wallace moved from the University of Utah to the University of Wisconsin to Harvard and finally to Stanford. As he recalls, "Since I was born in Iowa in 1909 (my hometown held me six weeks) I have lived in twenty places in eight different states, besides a couple of places in Canada, and in some of these places we lived in anywhere from two to ten different houses and neighborhoods."[3]

Later in life, as he tells us in the same essay, he found on several recent trips through Salt Lake City

> a conviction growing in me that I am not as homeless as I had thought. At worst, I had thought myself an Ishmael; at best, a half stranger in the city where I had lived the longest, a Gentile in the New Jerusalem.
>
> But a dozen years of absence from Zion, broken only by two or three short revisitings, have taught me different. I am as rich in a hometown as anyone, though I adopted my home as an adolescent and abandoned it as a young man.[4]

Thus Stegner belatedly acknowledged the strong and lasting influence Salt Lake City had on him.

Stegner's geographical rangings paralleled his career. Fiction writer, historian, biographer, editor, humanist, humanitarian, environmentalist, and essayist, he was a man in perpetual intellectual motion to the end of his life. He published twelve novels, three short-story collections, four histories, seven volumes of essays, and two biographies; he also edited several collections of stories and essays. As a mentor to young writers he nourished the early careers of people who came to make their mark on the American literary scene in the last half of the twentieth century: Edward Abbey, Wendell Berry, Robert Stone, Nancy Packard, Tillie Olson, Ken Kesey, Larry McMurtry, Scott Turow, and Ed McClanahan, to name just a few. As an environmentalist he wrote so effectively about the ecology of the West that he became almost a patron saint to conservationists.

Wallace Earle Stegner was born on February 18, 1909, on the farm of his maternal grandparents, Norwegian immigrants C. K. and Anne Paulson, near Lake Mills, Iowa (although the 1910 census lists his birthplace as Osnabrock, Cavalier County, northeastern North Dakota). His older brother, Cecil Lawrence, had been born in 1907. George Stegner was born in Henry County, western Illinois, just east of Rock Island and Moline, on September 25, 1879, to Lewis and Mary Stagner (probably a census taker's spelling error). A little more than a month later George took his wife and two sons back to Osnabrock, where George ran a pool hall and a speakeasy, or "blind pig." From there the family went to Washington State, where Hilda worked in a Seattle department store and had to place the two boys temporarily in a kind of orphans' home. George simply disappeared for a while before bringing the family to East End, Saskatchewan, close to the Alberta and Montana borders, where the family tried homesteading only to be burned out by a drought. The Canadian experience provided Stegner with much of the material for one of his finest works, *Wolf Willow: A History, a Story, and a Memory of the Last Plains Frontier* (1962). They then moved to Great Falls, Montana, where young Wallace mowed the lawn of Charles M. Russell, the famed western painter, and where for the first time young Wallace saw cement sidewalks, lawns, streetcars, hardwood floors, bathtubs, running water, and flush toilets: "It was incredible to me that only the day before we had lived in a world of privies and washbasins and slop buckets."[5]

In the summer of 1921 George Stegner moved his family to Salt Lake City and continued his activity as a bootlegger and operator of speakeasies in their homes around the city. Wallace and Cecil attended East High School, where Wallace made his mark as a scholar (with, among other studies, four years of Latin) and Cecil starred in athletics.

After graduation from East High School in 1925, Stegner entered the University of Utah, where he majored in English, edited the *Pen* literary magazine, played on the freshman basketball team, and played varsity tennis with David Freed, who went on to captain the American Davis Cup team in 1959–1961, when the Americans fought it out with the Australians, and to become a prominent Salt Lake attorney. Wallace's brother, Cecil, died of pneumonia at the age of twenty-three on January 27, 1930, leaving behind his wife, Elverna, and their young daughter, Carol. He is buried in the Salt Lake City Cemetery in the Park section, plot 37-6-5W.

Wallace received his bachelor of arts degree in 1930 and went on to get his master's and Ph.D. in 1935 at the University of Iowa with a dissertation on Clarence Edward Dutton, the American literary naturalist. While writing his dissertation, he took a part-time teaching job (four classes!) at Augustana College, a Lutheran liberal arts school in Rock Island, Illinois. The job turned out to be a disaster when he was fired. As he told Richard Etulain,

> I left Augustana when a big fight broke out between the Evangelicals who had hired me and the Fundamentalists who thought dangerous latitudinarian standards were being followed. I was, in effect, fired for being one, an atheist, two, an agnostic, three, an unbeliever in the principles of Christian higher education, and four, a nonbeliever in the Augsburg

Confession. Since I didn't see how I could be an atheist and an agnostic at the same time, and had never read the Augsburg Confession, and had not had the principles of higher Christian education explained to me, I was a sitting duck.[6]

While Stegner was doing doctoral work at Iowa, his mother died of breast cancer in Salt Lake City on September 27, 1933, at age fifty. She is buried next to Cecil and George in the Park section, plot 37-6-4W.

He took an instructorship at the University of Utah in the fall of 1934 and married Mary Page, a graduate student at Iowa, on September 1, 1934. Their son, Page, was born on January 31, 1937. While at Utah in 1936 he entered a short-novel contest sponsored by Little, Brown, the Boston publishing company, and on January 30, 1937, he received a telegram telling him that he had won the twenty-five hundred–dollar first prize (a princely sum, considering that his university salary was seventeen hundred dollars). With the university unable to promote and tenure him because of the Depression, he accepted an instructorship at the University of Wisconsin, but left in 1939 to take a position at Harvard.

On June 15, 1939, George Stegner killed himself and his lover, Dorothy Webb LeRoy, in the Hotel Heron in downtown Salt Lake. He was buried in the Salt Lake City Cemetery next to Hilda and Cecil, in the Park section, plot 37-6-3W, but unlike their graves his has no marker. Ironically, in Stegner's *Recapitulation*, Bruce Mason orders a marker for his father, Bo Mason. Mrs. LeRoy is buried in American Fork, Utah, about thirty miles south of Salt Lake City.

Looking back on his childhood and adolescence, Stegner had mixed feelings about his parents. In "Letter, Much Too Late," written to his mother more than fifty years after her death, he speaks of his father as

a husky, laughing, reckless, irreverent, storytelling charmer, a ballplayer, a fancy skater, a trapshooting champion, a pursuer of the main chance, a true believer in the American dream of something for nothing, a rolling stone who confidently expected to be eventually covered with moss. He was marking time between get-rich-quick schemes by running a "blind pig"—an illegal saloon. He offended every piety your father stood for. Perhaps that was why you married him, against loud protests from home.[7]

But for Stegner his mother was the "nester," a woman who desired nothing more than a settled home, children, neighbors, friends, a community. He says at one point in the same letter,

> But you must understand that you are the hardest sort of human character to make credible on paper. We are skeptical of kindness so unfailing, sympathy so instant and constant, trouble so patiently borne, forgiveness so wholehearted. Writing about you, I felt always on the edge of the unbelievable, as if I were writing a saint's life, or the legend of some Patient Griselda. I felt that I should warp you a little, give you some human failing or selfish motive; for saintly qualities, besides looking sentimental on the page, are a rebuke to those—and they are most of us—who have failed at them.
>
> What is more, saintly and long-suffering women tend to infuriate the current partisans of women's liberation, who look upon them as a masculine invention, the too submissive and too much praised victims of male dominance.[8]

In 1945 Stegner returned to the West when he took a position in the English Department at Stanford, where he assumed the directorship of the existing creative-writing program, the nation's finest, until his retirement. He retired from Stanford in 1971 out of disgust over academic politics in his department and the violence and classroom disruption generated by the antiwar movement.

Stegner was frequently honored: the Little, Brown prize in 1937, two O. Henry awards for the short story (1942 and 1950), three Guggenheim Fellowships (1950, 1952, and 1959), the gold medal of the Commonwealth Club of San Francisco (1967), the Pulitzer Prize for fiction for *Angle of Repose* (1972), the National Book Award for fiction for *The Spectator Bird* (1977), and the Robert Kirsch Award for Life Achievement from the *Los Angeles Times* (1980). He was also honored with honorary doctorates from the University of Utah (1968), the University of California (1969), Utah State University (1972), the University of Wisconsin (1986), Montana State University (1987), Ripon College (1989), and Middlebury College (1993).

During these years he was publishing at an astonishing rate. While at Wisconsin he published *The Potter's House* (1938) and at Harvard *On a Darkling Plain* (1940), *Fire and Ice* (1941), *Mormon Country* (1942), *The Big Rock Candy Mountain* (1943), and *One Nation* (1945).

From his years at Stanford came *Second Growth* (1947), *The Women on the Wall* (1950), *The Preacher and the Slave* (1950, later reprinted as *Joe Hill*), *Beyond the Hundredth Meridian: John Wesley Powell and the Second Opening of the West* (1954), *This Is Dinosaur* (1956), *The City of the Living, and Other Stories* (1956), *Wolf Willow* (1962), *The Gathering of Zion: The Story of the Mormon Trail* (1964), *All the Little Live Things* (1967), and *The Sound of Mountain Water* (1969).

After his retirement from Stanford he produced *Angle of Repose* (1971), *Discovery: The Search for Arabian Oil* (1971), *The Uneasy Chair: A Biography of Bernard DeVoto* (1974), *The Letters of Bernard DeVoto* (editor, 1975), *The Spectator Bird* (1976), *Recapitulation* (1979), *American Places* (1981, with Page Stegner and photographs by Eliot Porter), *One Way to Spell Man* (1982), *Conversations with Wallace Stegner on Western History and Literature* (1982, interviews with Richard Etulain), *Crossing to Safety* (1987), *The American West as Living Space* (1987), *Collected Stories of Wallace Stegner* (1990), and *Where the Bluebird Sings to the Lemonade Springs: Living and Writing in the West* (1992).

While in Santa Fe, New Mexico, to receive an award from the Mountain and Plains Booksellers Association, Stegner was critically injured in an automobile accident on March 28, 1993, and he died on April 13. Part of his ashes were spread at Baker Hill in Vermont, close to the home he had purchased years before and where he and Mary had spent many of their summers.

At the time of his death Stegner was considered by many to be the finest western writer of the twentieth century. All of his work—whether fiction, criticism, history, biography, or environmental writing—still fascinates a wide and appreciative audience, and most of it remains in print. This is so, perhaps, because all of it is marked by a compassionate concern for the human condition. His fiction gives us characters who face real human problems and react to them in recognizably human ways. As James Hepworth has said in his essay "Wallace Stegner: The Quiet Revolutionary," the people in Stegner's fiction

> do not challenge or defy the universe, much less despair of it. They do confront its mystery, suffer spiritual uncertainties and embarrassments, attempt reconciliations, and reconstruct values commonly forgotten, lost, or repudiated. They move by trial and error towards dubious ends, but then that is the law of nature. Their dreams are all American dreams: not of something for nothing, but of a chance at life, safety, home, and belonging. Their questions arise from anguish and spiritual uncertainty, for they seek to impose order on their own lives, to give themselves and others meaning, purpose, direction.[9]

This same compassion is shown in "Born a Square," an essay published in 1964, in which Stegner expresses his annoyance with much of modern fiction produced by "a literary generation that appears to specialize in despair, hostility, hypersexuality, and disgust," and gives us fiction filled with "despair, decadence, masochism, sadism, self-pity, anger, and the hopeless prick of conscience."[10]

WALLACE STEGNER'S SALT LAKE CITY

In 1945 he published *One Nation,* a book two decades ahead of the civil rights movement, in which he deals sympathetically with the problems of African Americans, American Indians, Latinos, Asians, Catholics, and Jews. And in *Wolf Willow* he deplores the brutal treatment of American Indians: "No one who has studied western history can cling to the belief that the Nazis invented genocide. Extermination was a doctrine accepted widely, both officially and unofficially, in the western United States after the Civil War."[11]

Although Stegner made it clear that his primary writing focus was fiction, he was always very much concerned with the quality of American life. In numerous essays and several books, in his successful opposition to the building of a dam system in Dinosaur National Monument in northeastern Utah and northwestern Colorado, and in his concern about water problems in the West, he believed that the preservation of our air, water, land, and wilderness resources is a precious and priceless legacy to our children and our children's children, a heritage he describes in "Coda: Wilderness Letter" as "the geography of hope."[12]

His significance in American culture has been recognized with honorary doctorates, the establishment of the Wallace Stegner Chair of History at Montana State University, and the development of the Wallace Stegner Center for Land, Resources, and the Environment in the S. J. Quinney College of Law at the University of Utah, where a Stegner environmental conference is held every spring. His papers, in 179 boxes, and his typewriter are in the Special Collections section of the University of Utah's J. Willard Marriott Library.

More than a dozen years after his death, his reputation in American literature is somewhat unclear. Revered by readers and scholars in the western United States as one of the major American writers of the twentieth century, he is still unknown to a large segment of the reading public who seem to prefer writers who do not rise to his eminence. But few of the modern American fiction writers taught in college and university classrooms can match his concern for people. Leonard McDonald, a supporting character in *A Shooting Star* (1961), perhaps expresses the philosophy that permeates all of Stegner's work: "I'll tell you what I believe in. I believe in human love and human kindness and human responsibility.... The only revolution that interests me is one that will give more people more comprehension of their human possibilities and their human obligations." And in "Born a Square" Stegner says that "some part of our most advertised fiction is sick, out of its mind, and out of the moral world, worshipful of Moloch, in love with decay and death. Another part is simply the corrupt answer to a corrupt demand, which is in turn cynically promoted. I do not mean 'dirty' words or forthright scenes, sexual or otherwise; I speak of a necrophilic playing with despair, which is nothing to be played with."[13] This humane approach to literature and society places Stegner squarely in the great tradition of literature from the classics to the present.

Even though he "adopted [his] home as an adolescent and abandoned it as a young man," Stegner never left Salt Lake City behind. In three novels, several short stories, and a number of essays he drew upon the city for settings, scenes, characters, and reminiscences. The latter third of *The Big Rock Candy Mountain,* all of *Recapitulation,* and parts of *Joe Hill, Mormon Country,* and *The Gathering of Zion* take place in Salt Lake. Stegner also used the city as setting for several short stories that he later incorporated (with changes of various sorts) into three short stories: "The Volunteer," "The Blue-Winged Teal," and "Maiden in a Tower." Two autobiographical essays, "At Home in the Fields of the Lord" and "It Is the Love of Books I Owe Them," tell of his growing up as a non-Mormon boy in Salt Lake City and his years at the University of Utah. There is also the autobiographical-historical essay "Xanadu by the Salt Flats," which deals with the history of Saltair, the popular resort by the Great Salt Lake that flourished in the late nineteenth and early twentieth centuries where Stegner worked during one of his high school summers. In *Mormon Country* and *The Gathering of Zion: The Story of the Mormon Trail,* he used the city for cultural and historical focus.

Throughout his works dealing with Salt Lake City, Stegner mentions many places for one purpose or another. There are businesses such as the Hotel

Utah and its Sky Room restaurant, the Temple Square Hotel, the Night Owl Inn, the Old Mill Inn, Bill Winder's bookstore, Joe Vincent's Café, Utah Woolen Mills, the Deseret Gymnasium, and the Brigham Street Pharmacy. There are the schools such as East High and the University of Utah; institutions such as the Utah State Prison, which had been located in the Sugar House area of Salt Lake City; and streets such as 700 East, 1300 East, South Temple, Main Street, State Street, and Foothill Drive.

In his fiction Stegner drew upon not only the places of Salt Lake City of the 1920s and 1930s but also the people he knew during his years there: teachers, professors, classmates, athletic teammates. The people are often lightly disguised, and their real-life models can be determined with some certainty. The places he used for settings are also often identifiable, although occasionally either his memory failed him as to an exact location or he took literary license. In *Recapitulation,* for example, he has Bruce Mason driving past Liberty Park on "Seventh South" instead of 700 East (700 South is two blocks north of the park), and Bruce later watches the storm approach from "Long Peak" instead of Lone Peak.[14]

But as Stegner told his biographer Jackson L. Benson, we have to be very careful about reading everything in *The Big Rock Candy Mountain, Recapitulation,* and the Salt Lake short stories as being completely autobiographical. In a letter to Benson on August 24, 1987, he said that in assuming that all of his characters are taken from real life, the reader is

> on very boggy ground, like a floating island in the Okefenokee Swamp. In all of those cases I took hints from reality. In all of them I so manipulated the reality that none of those people, except maybe my mother, would recognize the character on the page. And though it might be intriguing to the kind of reader who thinks that the way to assume that *Recapitulation* is the record of my broken heart smashed by a faithless babe, it would be dangerously inaccurate, and unjust both to those "originals" and to me....

There are very few episodes in *Recapitulation* that come from reality (including all the romantic scenes and the Mormon wedding), except the circumstances of how I happened to get sent off by pure accident to graduate school. The people are in the novel because the novel demanded them, not because I so vividly remembered them that I had to put them in.[15]

And in an interview with Richard Etulain regarding *The Big Rock Candy Mountain,* Stegner said,

> I was drawing on my own experience a lot, but also let me repeat what I've said here, that the book isn't all personal experience. And even when you do draw on your experience you don't have to write autobiography. Somewhere or other, I think in *Recapitulation,* I remark that the memory can be an artist as well as a historian. You draw on it, but you don't draw on it literally. You draw on it all the time. I don't suppose you can do anything else but draw on your own experience, in the same way you can only imagine what you have seen. You can't imagine creatures you haven't seen.[16]

This book is an attempt to show something of the environment in which Stegner lived for about fourteen years. The photographs reflect the Salt Lake City of the 1920s and 1930s in which he survived and rose above a very difficult home situation, was educated, grew to manhood, and began his career as a writer and teacher.

As we look back on Stegner's distinguished career, we might keep in mind the judgment made by Jackson Benson, paraphrasing Robert Stone's comment on his mentor at Stanford:

Wallace Stegner believed all those things we used to believe in. He was a remarkable man, not the least remarkable in making his life and work of one piece. His integrity shone forth equally in both. He was not stern, self-righteous, or judgmental, but was a person who could be the life of the party, someone who knew how to have fun and who had a ready sense of humor.

Yet he was unbending in his belief in right conduct. He was kind, thoughtful, and generous, a person who was easy to talk to, yet he was held almost in awe by many who knew him as being somewhat larger than life, in the expectations he had for himself and in his superhuman capacity for work.[17]

For Wallace Stegner Salt Lake City proved to be not only a place that formed his character and widened his intellectual and literary horizons but also one whose people and places engraved themselves onto his artistic memory.

East High School

WHEN STEGNER CAME TO SALT LAKE CITY in 1921, he first attended South Junior High School at 1245 South State and then moved on to East High School on 1300 East 900 South. The family was living at 873 East 400 South after moving from their first home at 1191 South 700 East and their second at 1901 South State.

When Stegner entered East High in 1925, the building was eleven years old, having been completed in 1914. The enrollment was about thirteen hundred. The principal was Alice E. Row, the vice principal DeVoe Woolf. The faculty numbered sixty-one in 1927, according to the 1927 *Eastonia,* the East High yearbook. In that same year the school offered courses in art, chemistry, math, mechanical drawing, German, French, Spanish, English, speech, dramatics, history, Latin, social science, science, physics, biology, cooking, sewing and millinery, design, psychology, and commerce.

During their three years at East High, Wallace and Cecil took part in many student activities. Because Wallace had skipped two grades (one in East End, Saskatchewan, and one in Salt Lake), they graduated together in 1925 when Wallace was sixteen and Cecil seventeen. Stegner uses their graduation for a descriptive passage in *The Big Rock Candy Mountain* as Chet (Cecil) thinks about his own experiences at the school:

33

Then graduation, he and Bruce [Wallace] graduating together, the assembly hall full of parents and all the little high school girls running around halls and lawns in their first formals, the long meeting when you sat and waited your turn to go up on the stage and get your football sweater.

… That was the end of school, of stinking chem., of lab physics classes where you experimented with the laws of the pendulum, swinging plumb-bobs on strings down the stairwell from the third floor to the basement, so that girls going in the door of the girls' gym could be bopped with them. Now was the end of practices after school, of showers in the steamy old shower room and towel fights between the lockers, of snake dances through the streets to celebrate victories, of operas in the old Salt Lake Theater where you sang tenor leads in *Mademoiselle Modiste* or *The Red Mill.* This was the end of lunches on the lawn while the gulls flew over crying, of butts snitched behind the corner of Mad Maisie's, of hot dogs and mustard and rootbeer over her messy counter…. Bruce said he was going on to college. Let him be the grind of the family. There was more fun in the world than that.[1]

"Mad Maisie's" is very likely a name created by Stegner for a lunchroom at the corner of 1245 East 800 South run by an Alice Miller, as shown in the 1925 city directory. Also listed at the same address is a Mrs. Mary Miller. By 1929, however, the lunchroom was apparently gone, for it is no longer listed in the directory, although Alice Miller is simply listed as a householder. A number of older Salt Lake residents remember the place, which they say was known by their generation as "Marijuana Mary's." Another lunchroom appears in the 1929 directory, this one known as East Side Lunch, at 863 South 1300 East, which would have been right across the street to the east from the high school, but the location does not fit the location in the novel.

Cecil, known as "Steg," starred on the football, basketball, and baseball teams. He was also in the Rifle Club, the Spanish Club, and something called the 4-T Club. He was a sergeant in the Reserve Officers' Training Corps (ROTC), and participated in opera during his junior and senior years. As Stegner says in his conversations with Richard Etulain, Cecil's activities in high school were almost all associated with athletics: "He wasn't much of a scholar. On the other hand, he was a singer. He had a good tenor voice, and he used to be in all local operettas. He was a kind of activities man, where I was the grind."[2]

Wallace was on the basketball team during his junior year, served as president of the Latin Club and participated in the Chemistry Club as a senior, was a second lieutenant in the ROTC, and was on the business staff of the school newspaper, the *Red and Black*. During his freshman year he took two semesters each of geometry, English, zoology, Latin, hygiene, and gym. The next year he studied physics, algebra, Latin, English, ROTC drill, gym, solid geometry, and physics. In his third year he studied ancient history, Latin, English, chemistry, hygiene, gym, ROTC, and civics. As might be expected, his grades were very high.

Of his years at East High, Stegner has written in "Finding the Place: A Migrant Childhood":

> What I most wanted, it seems to me now, was to belong to something, and Mormon institutions were made to order for belongers. Once in the Boy Scouts, I went up through the ranks like smoke up a chimney. I was a demon activist in school Latin clubs and dramatic societies (I played saucy bellhops and brattish boys). In my first year at East High School I was desolated because they wouldn't let me into ROTC, which was compulsory for boys, because I didn't weigh a hundred pounds. Attempting to work out the angles, I tried out for the rifle team and made it, assuming that then they would have to let me in. Instead, they barred me from

competing because I wasn't a member of the ROTC. By overeating and muscling bricks I made it over the hundred-pound mark by the next year, and went through the ranks the way I had gone through the ranks of the Boy Scouts—corporal to sergeant, sergeant to first sergeant, first sergeant to second lieutenant, second lieutenant to first lieutenant. I had my moment of glory when, in Sam Browne belt, leather puttees, shoulder pips, and sword, I led a platoon down Main Street in the Decoration Day parade.

Then in my senior year, between the ages of fifteen and sixteen, I grew six inches. It was like a graduation, more important to me than graduation from high school, and the beginning of the happiest years I ever knew or ever will know. Suddenly I was big enough to hold my own in sports. Suddenly I had friends who looked on me as an equal and not as a mascot. Suddenly, at the University of Utah, I was playing on the freshman basketball team and a little later on the tennis team. Suddenly I was being rushed by a fraternity, and acquired brothers, and a secret grip, and a book of tong songs. Beatitude.

Cecil, on the other hand, was at best an indifferent student with failures—F's in second-year English, second-year hygiene, first-year Latin, and first-year Spanish, and geometry, but in most other subjects his grades were in the C+ to B range.[3]

In none of his semiautobiographical novels, short stories, or essays does Stegner make as much use of his years at East High as he does those at the university or the geographical environment of Salt Lake City. Aside from Cecil, the only characters to come out of his high school experiences are the Latin teachers in *Recapitulation* and the short story "The Volunteer." In the novel young Bruce wants to impress his teacher:

When his Latin teacher said she had always wanted a scale model of a Roman *castra* so that pupils reading Caesar's *Gallic Wars* could see exactly how the legions built their defenses, of course Bruce volunteered.... "A *castra*? I'll make one!" he said. "I know a slough where there's good clay. I'll get some tonight after school."

"Now that, Bruce," said Miss Van Vliet, "is the spirit I like to see."[4]

In "The Volunteer," Stegner uses a first-person point of view and changes the name of the teacher:

When my Latin teacher said she had always wanted a scale model of a Roman *castra* so that pupils reading about the campaign against the Helvetians could see exactly how the legions built their defenses, of course I volunteered. I was always volunteering. The year must have been 1922. I was thirteen years old, two years behind myself in physical growth, two years ahead of myself in school. Around the high school I drew two kinds of attention, one kind from teachers and another from boys, especially big boys and most especially stupid ones. The last I ignored, or tried to, and I cultivated the praise of teachers, which was easy to win. Nevertheless, I suppose I would have given considerable to be big and stupid so that I too could sneer at my little peaked face focused on the teacher ready to cry answers, and my little skinny arm flapping at every call to duty.[5]

The next two paragraphs of the story are word for word the same, except that the Latin teacher's name is changed to Van Der Fleet. In both narratives Bruce goes out into the cold night in late November to a slough near Seventeenth South and Fifth East in the novel, but the location is not mentioned in the story. In both narratives he comes home, wet and cold and muddy, to find his father entertaining the slovenly Lew McReady (a married man) and his lover with illegal drinks.[6]

It seems very likely that Stegner drew upon his memories of a high school Latin teacher for Van Vliet and Van Der Fleet. Stegner took six Latin courses from Marion Van Pelt (1889–1965), who continued to teach at East until the mid-1950s. She is buried in the Mount Olivet Cemetery near the University of Utah.

One of the best passages anywhere in Stegner's writing is one from *Recapitulation,* in which Bruce Mason walks back from the funeral home with a box left to him by his deceased aunt. It describes not only the Bruce Mason of the East High and university years but also most adolescent males:

> He knew this Bruce Mason who walked down South Temple Street carrying a cardboard box of his aunt's unwanted leavings. He had lived with him a long time, he knew what he could do and how he would respond to different situations. But Bruce Mason walked double. Inside him, walking with the same muscles and feeling with the same nerves and sweating through the same pores, went a thin brown youth, volatile, impulsive, never at rest, not so much a person as a possibility, or a bundle of possibilities: subject to enthusiasm and elation and exuberance and occasional great black moods, stubborn, capable of scheming but often astonished by consequences, a boy vulnerable to wonder, awe, worship, devotion, hatred, guilt, vanity, shame, ambition, dreams, treachery; a boy avid for acceptance and distinction, secretive and a blabbermouth, life-crazy and hence girl-crazy, a show-off who could be withered by a contemptuous word or look, a creature overflowing with brash self-confidence one minute and oppressed by its own worthlessness the next; a vessel of primary sensations undiluted by experience, wisdom, or fatigue.[7]

At one point in *The Big Rock Candy Mountain,* Bruce thinks about his experiences during his high school years:

There was school to take Bruce's time, there was the constant impatient agonized wish that he would ever start growing, get some muscle, get to be an athlete like Chet. There was the habit of walking tiptoe all the way to school to develop his calves, the secret exercises in the basement to harden his neck and arms. There were his envy and pride, oddly mixed, when Chet did something spectacular and got his name in the papers, and his moral horror when he found that Chet and all his gang of big-chested boys smoked cigarettes and played penny ante poker.[8]

Much of *The Big Rock Candy Mountain*'s Salt Lake City section, however, deals at some length with Chet's athletic prowess and success, his starring in newspaper sports-page headlines and stories, and his unfortunate courtship and marriage.

One of the more memorable experiences for Stegner was his participation in the Citizens' Military Training Camp at Fort Douglas during summer vacation. The CMTC, as it was known, was established by Congress in 1920 in the National Defense Act. As the *CMTC: Fort Douglas, 1938* booklet shows, the CMTC enrolled more than a half-million young men ages seventeen to twenty-four nationwide during its eighteen years of existence. The mission of the CMTC was "to bring together young men of high type from all sections of the country and thereby develop closer national and social unity; to teach the privileges, duties, and responsibilities of American citizenship; to stimulate patriotism; to interest young men in the importance of military training; to teach self-discipline and obedience; and to develop the physical standard of American youth through participation in military exercises, athletic games and sports, conducted under expert directors." The course ran for four summers: the Basic the first summer and the Red, White, and Blue courses the remaining three. At the end of the fourth the graduates could apply for a second lieutenant's commission in the U.S. Army. Each camp, like the one at Fort Douglas, was staffed by army personnel: a commanding officer (a major), a chaplain (a lieutenant colonel), an adjutant (a captain), a second lieutenant, and a number of noncommissioned officers.[9] One can easily imagine the extreme discomfort of the students as they drilled under the hot Utah sun in heavy woolen uniforms, campaign hats, and puttees declared by the army as surplus from World War I, as were their rifles and other equipment. The surplus continued to be used until the end of the program at the beginning of World War II.

Stegner used his experiences at the Fort Douglas CMTC (it's not clear whether he spent more than one summer there) for a scene in *Recapitulation:*

> The first day on the pistol range, he found that he could not lift the boxes of ammunition that the others picked up and staggered off with. Couldn't budge them, they might as well have been bolted to the ground. Then at the weekly parade and inspection, he got dizzy in the heat and threw up, splashing those next to him in line. The sergeant took one disgusted look and told him to fall out and go somewhere and stay the hell out of the way. He spent the rest of the morning under a tree at the edge of the parade ground watching his fellows sweat out there in their woolen uniforms. He knew exactly what they thought of him, and he agreed.
>
> The whole miserable camp went that way. In the second week they had a sham battle. He was stringing field telephone lines, and he got fouled up and didn't get them to the command post in time, so that the whole apricot orchard held by the Blues was overrun. Everybody knew who was responsible. And a while after that, on the pistol range again, Bruce had just reloaded and was standing at raise pistol after shooting 68 out of 70 possible at twenty-five yards, and the colonel was standing by him giving him his astonished commendation when Bruce's index finger, which should have been up along the barrel of the .45 automatic, accidentally wandered inside the trigger guard.

The gun went off right beside his ear; and almost in the colonel's face. When Bruce could see again, and the colonel had recovered from his leap backward, Bruce saw that he had shot a scallop out of the brim of the colonel's hat. The colonel gave him such a scared, furious bawling-out—exactly like Bruce's father, he sounded—that Bruce lay awake most of the night trying to choose between desertion and suicide.

All he got out of camp was some sharpshooter medals, rifle and pistol.[10]

Stegner's adolescence, as he says in "At Home in the Fields of Lord," gave him "most of the usual anguishes and some rather special ones besides. Certainly some of the years I lived in Salt Lake City were the most miserable years of my life, with their share of death and violence and more than their share of fear, and I am sure now that off and on and for considerable periods I can hardly have been completely sane."[11]

Stegner's years at East High School indeed may have been affected by a home situation marked by tension between a criminal, abusive father and a loving, nest-seeking mother, and by his own typical adolescent uncertainties and insecurities. But the school gave him opportunities not only to make his mark and to prepare him for further education and his career as a writer and humanitarian but also to draw upon his experiences and friends for fiction.

The University of Utah

WHEN WALLACE STEGNER STARTED CLASSES there in September
1925, the University of Utah was a small campus centered around
what is today called the Presidents' Circle. A return to the campus of eighty years
ago would surprise everyone regarding the growth of the campus, for in Stegner's
undergraduate years there was little beyond the twenty-five buildings around and
near the circle. Sydney Angleman, who came to the university in 1927 and served
as a professor of English and in several administrative positions, in his fine essay,
"Gone the Meadowlarks," once described the campus as he first saw it:

> The four original buildings and the Park Building were the center of the
> campus. To the west the broad lawns sloped down to University Street.
> To the east, behind the Park Building and its small parking lot (parking
> was then no problem except for lovers and smokers seeking shelter from
> [Dean] Aunt Lucy VanCott's vigilant eye), stretched the empty fields of
> Fort Douglas, lovely with the sound of meadowlarks in the spring, where
> one could gather delicious mushrooms if he knew the right spot and the
> right kind. In the little stream that cut across the main path, Professor
> Ernest Pehrson, that legendary fisherman, once caught a trout with his
> bare hands. In the spring too, the circle would one day come alight as
> the great cherries flung their masses of white against the dark shadows of
> the spruces, and a receptive English student, dreaming at the window of

the "L" Building [now the LeRoy Cowles Building] would suddenly find Housman's "Loveliest of Trees" take life before his eyes.[1]

The campus in 1926, as Professor Angleman pointed out, consisted of thirty-four departments in six schools (Arts and Sciences, Business, Education, Engineering and Mines, Law, and a two-year medical school). The faculty numbered 180, of whom 22 percent held a doctorate.

A decade earlier, Utah-born Bernard DeVoto, who later became one of America's leading historians and social critics, and who would become Stegner's mentor and close friend (as well as the subject of Stegner's biography), attended the university for one year. But DeVoto moved east to Harvard when the university was plagued by President Joseph T. Kingsbury's firing of four professors (one in physics, one in modern languages, and two in English), and the subsequent black-listing of the university by the American Association of University Professors (the first time the organization sanctioned a college or university).

As the university catalogs from 1925 through 1937 show, the enrollment during Stegner's years was also small. In his freshman year the university had a total of 2,910 students (2,805 undergraduate and 105 graduate). In 1927 the university graduated 314 students with bachelor's degrees and fifteen with master's. In his last student year the enrollment had grown to 3,317 (3,232 undergraduate and 85 graduate). When he returned to teach in the fall of 1934, the enrollment had grown to 3,677 (3,481 undergraduate and 196 graduate). Three years later, in Stegner's last faculty year, the undergraduates numbered 3,784, the graduates 150, for a total of 3,934, with an additional 737 in summer school. In 1935, in Stegner's second year of teaching, the library held 124,070 bound volumes.[2] The university's enrollment now is nearly 29,000, and the J. Willard Marriott Library and its campus affiliates in law and health sciences now have more than 3 million volumes.

During these years the campus began to expand. In 1927 Ute Stadium for football and track was completed, with seating for 20,000 fans. The School of Mines Building opened in 1929, the Union Building (later the Music Building, now the David P. Gardner Hall) and Kingsbury Hall in 1931, and the George Thomas Library in 1935. The university gained room for expansion in 1934 when it received sixty-one acres from the Fort Douglas military reservation. Before these additions the Park Building contained the library on its third floor; the student union and the bookstore were on the ground level.

Leading the university during Stegner's years was Dr. George Thomas, born in 1866 to Welsh immigrant parents in Hyde Park, Cache County. He attended Brigham Young Academy in Logan and went on to receive a summa cum laude bachelor's degree, and later a master's, from Harvard. Later he studied at the Universities of Paris, Berlin, and Halle, receiving a Ph.D. from the latter in 1909. In his early professional years he served as principal of Ogden High School, as professor of English at Brigham Young College, and as professor of history and economics at the Utah State Agricultural College (now Utah State University). In 1919 he came to the University of Utah as a professor of economics and acting dean of the College of Commerce. He was inaugurated as president on April 5, 1922, and he served until November 15, 1940.[3] As an indication of the times, the university's budget for 1927–1928 was $800,000.[4]

The dean of arts and sciences was James L. Gibson, who came to the university in 1904 as a professor of mathematics after getting master's degrees from Columbia and Cambridge. In 1915 he became dean.[5]

Surprising to modern university students would be the entrance and graduation requirements and the cost of tuition and fees, as published in the university's catalogs. In 1925, for example, students applying for entrance with fewer than 25 hours of high school French, German, Greek, Latin, or Spanish would have to make up the difference at the university. For graduation 183 quarter hours were required, with no more than 60 in any one department. Graduation requirements for all students included English 1a, 1b, and 1c; Hygiene 1; Physical Education 2, 3, and 4 (or Military Science and Tactics 1, 2, and 3); and 13 hours from each of the following groups: Mathematics and Physical Science, Biological Science, Social Science, and Language (Ancient, Modern, and Public Speaking). The university offered six degrees: bachelor of arts, bachelor of science, master of arts, master of science, master of science in engineering, and bachelor of laws.

In 1925 the tuition for Utah residents was $13.00 per quarter ($35.00 for nonresidents), plus a $10.00 annual registration fee and class fees of $0.75 per quarter for juniors and seniors and $0.50 for freshmen and sophomores. By 1935, when Stegner was teaching at the university, the resident tuition and fees had risen to $40.75 for the fall quarter, $26.25 for the winter, and $25.50 for the spring.

Despite the rigors of their course work and off-campus responsibilities, students at the university had their fun, as reflected in two items from the "Bull Pen" section of the 1927 *Utonian:*

THE STUDENT BODY

We think as we are told to think,
And expect everyone else to do the same—
We are abominably educated.
We have no conception of art
And no comprehension of it.
We have no sense of form,
No sense of harmony,
No sense of beauty,
And no sense of humor.
We are responsive to everything except thought.
We believe in everything except the worthwhile.
But on the whole we are very tolerant:
We can forgive everything except intelligence.
We are the student body.

And from a fictional coed named Levina Dingbat:

I was an ardent seeker of culture:
As a consequence I was exposed to lectures on
Enzymes,
Streptococci,
Chiropractic,
Ethnography,
Spontaneous generation,
Osteopathy,
Fletcherism,
Spiritualism, and
The New Thought.
Professors assailed me with
Greek,
Latin,
German,
French,
Italian,
Cuneiform Script,
Hieroglyphics,
The Signs of the Magi, and
The formulae of the English Department.
After four years, I received a degree (cum laude)
And married a Ford salesman.[6]

The 1931 *Utonian* could also satirize the sororities and fraternities. Lamda Phi Lamda, for example, was supposed to stand for "Love Fat Ladies" with the motto "Hell, Harold, I can't dance in these tight ___" (blank in original). Sigma

Nu, Stegner's fraternity, was supposedly founded by "the man without a country in a cemetery on a very dark night." Its meaning was "Sensuous Neurotics," its password "Let's give a party for some sorority," and its motto "Spread that Sigma Nuer." University faculties have always been the butts of student satire, and those of Stegner's years at the university suffered, too, as shown in the 1931 *Utonian:* "Another group of mugs hired by the state to annoy the students is the faculty. Look them over sometime and you will agree that a better bunch of enjoyment murderers never lived. Some of them expect you to come to class. And there is a bunch over in the Departments of English and History who expect you to stay awake as they strangle the classics and get tangled up in the events of bygone days. Ignore them if possible and get your sleep anyway."[7]

Despite student jokes about the university, its academics, and its social life, the school was beginning to make its presence known in the wider world when Phi Beta Kappa's Alpha of Utah Chapter was installed in January 1935 with Professor L. A. Quivey of the English Department as president.[8]

Outside the classroom the students of the 1920s and 1930s kept themselves busy with athletics (football, basketball, track and field, polo, and others), publications (the *Utah Chronicle, Humbug, Pen,* and *Utonian*), seven fraternities and eight sororities, and numerous professional and fraternal groups for students majoring in business, journalism, literature, medicine, law, chemistry, drama, physical education, engineering, and debate.

Stegner majored in English, and although the department was not as well known as it was to be later, it had a solid faculty. In 1925, when he matriculated, the department had fourteen members, only two of whom—George M. Marshall (Litt.D.) and Vardis Fisher (Ph.D.)—held a doctorate. In these years the department brought in young faculty who continued at Utah as late as the early 1970s: Myrtle Austin (1924–1965), Dorothy Snow (1924–1970), Lester Hubbard (1925–1960), Elsie Rohrbaugh (1925–1960), Sydney Angleman (1927–1971), Robert

Crabtree (1927–1964), Louis Zucker (1928–1963), Edward Chapman (1929–1966), Gretchen Horst (1929–1953), and Brewster Ghiselin (1929–1971).

Several of these people became Stegner's lifetime friends. The Wallace Stegner Collection in the J. Willard Marriott Library at the University of Utah contains correspondence with Angleman and his wife, Mildred, from 1938 to 1977 and with Chapman from 1939 to 1947. And when he came back to Salt Lake City for various events (book signings, speeches, and the dedication of the Marriott Library), Stegner spent a great deal of time with faculty, colleagues, classmates, and former students.

These faculty were for him a special type not easily found among university professors of later decades. Like Sherman Brown Neff, who was head of the English Department during most of Stegner's time at the university, his professors were not "of that more recent tribe who infest the English departments and do their best to make students feel superior to what they read."[9]

Stegner's years as an undergraduate produced a number of people who went on to distinguished careers. President Gordon B. Hinckley of the Church of Jesus Christ of Latter-day Saints majored in English and graduated in 1932. Obert C. Tanner, philanthropist and scholar, took his bachelor's degree in 1929 and later a law degree. David Freed, Stegner's teammate on the Utah tennis team and later captain of the American Davis Cup tennis team, became a prominent attorney and civic leader. J. Milton "Red" Cowan, perhaps Stegner's closest friend, took his B.A. and M.A. at Utah 1931 and 1932 and his Ph.D. at Iowa before becoming a distinguished professor of languages and linguistics, first at Iowa and later at Cornell, and the author of books on linguistics. Also at Utah during Stegner's students years was Phyllis McGinley, who edited the student *Pen* magazine (a position Stegner later held), graduated in 1927, and went on to a career as a distinguished poet who won the Pulitzer Prize for Poetry in 1961 for *Times Three: Selected Verse from Three Decades* and was featured in a cover article of *Time* for June 18, 1965, and in an earlier article in the same magazine on July 19, 1964.[10]

Among others at the university during Stegner's student years were G. Homer Durham, who distinguished himself as a faculty member at Utah, administrator at several western universities, and president of Arizona State University; Maurine Whipple, who published the distinguished and prizewinning novel *The Giant Joshua;* Allan Crockett, later chief justice of the Utah Supreme Court; Reva Beck Bosone, who became Utah's first elected judge and the state's first congresswoman; J. Willard and Alice Sheets Marriott, who founded the Hot Shoppe Restaurants and the Marriott Hotels; Kendall Garff, prominent in politics and auto dealerships; Preston Summerhays, famous in athletic and coaching circles; Calvin Behle, one of the founders of the law firm of Parsons, Behle, and Latimer; James D. Moyle, prominent attorney; and F. Henry Henroid, later chief justice of the Utah Supreme Court.

But when Stegner and his friends graduated in the spring of 1930, America was slipping fast into the Depression. As John S. McCormick has pointed out, at the beginning of 1930, only a few months after Black Friday in 1929, some 8,700 Utah workers were unemployed, as were 36,000 in 1931 and 61,500 in 1932 (the latter 35.8 percent of the workforce).[11]

In *Recapitulation* and the two essays here reprinted, as well as in his conversations with Richard Etulain, Stegner mentions dozens of people, both real and imagined, and as many places. In the essays and conversations he mentions faculty friends at the University of Utah. In addition to the English faculty, he writes about friends such as Juanita Crawford, Helen "Peg" Foster, Lyn Crone, Evert "Hap" Lybbert, Stan Rock, Ray Forsberg, Red Cowan, Jack Irvine, Mel Gallagher, Jim Gilbert, Ernest "Baldy" Simkins, Chick Blevens, Met Wilson, and Ted Aldous.[12]

Stegner's undergraduate career at the university is perhaps best summarized by a paragraph in his essay "Finding the Place: A Migrant Childhood":

> In the middle of my freshman year I got a job working afternoons and
> Saturdays in a floor-coverings store, at twenty-five cents an hour, and with

financial independence achieved, began to date girls who a year earlier had looked over my head. The success of my transition from have-not to have was measured by my grades: straight A's as a freshman, straight B's as a sophomore. My companions included a few intellectuals; most were card-players, beer drinkers and jocks. My long-term addiction to books, which had been intensified by access to the Carnegie Library on State Street, suffered. My literary ambitions, which had been stimulated by the novelist Vardis Fisher, my freshman English instructor, got shelved. I was almost glad that Fisher left after my first year, for he had a caustic tongue and a great contempt for time-wasters. Just the same, I wouldn't have traded by newly achieved life as an insider for an introduction to Clara Bow.[13]

As he was to say in the essay about his university days, the four undergraduate years and the three as a faculty member, "for all its easy-going atmosphere, and despite all my apparent effort to avoid contamination by ideas, the University did reach me. It reached me early and it continued to reach me, often when I didn't know it was doing so."[14]

All his life Stegner was interested in athletics, although he did not match the athletic skills of his brother Cecil. At the university he played on the freshman basketball team and lettered in tennis during his sophomore, junior, and senior years. The 1931 *Utonian* reported that during the previous tennis season he "had improved his game considerably at the year went on...and is the possessor of a forehand loop drive that finds the corners of the court with unerring accuracy." Stegner is listed with David Freed, Jack Irvine, and Harry Guss as Ute tennis players who "loom as possible champions in the near future" in the Rocky Mountain area along with former Utes Mel Gallagher and Chick Blevins. During his final season in matches with Utah State and Brigham Young Universities, Stegner lost in singles to Wes Porter and with Ross Sutton in doubles lost to BYU's Porter and Kent Johnson. In the match with Utah State, Stegner teamed with Harold Smith to defeat Hy Cannon and Edward Swinyard, but he lost to Cannon in the singles match. In a return match with BYU Stegner and Smith beat Eldon Brimley and Kent Johnson.[15]

And given his interest in tennis and baseball, we can assume that he followed the Utes in football and basketball as well. Ute Stadium opened for football in 1927 with seating for 20,000, the largest in the state. Under Coach Ike Armstrong, the Utes were 58-16-3 from 1925 through 1936 (Armstrong went on to compile a 141-55-15 record before he left the university after the 1949 season), won four Rocky Mountain Conference (RMC) Championships, and had a 9-0-1 record against BYU (outscoring the Cougars 302-27). In 1928–1930 the team won sixteen straight games, a record finally broken at eighteen in 2003–2005 by the Utes of coaches Urban Meyer and Kyle Whittingham.

In basketball the Utes had a winning record but were not nearly so successful. Under Ike Armstrong (1925–1927) and Vadal Peterson (1927 onward) they had only four winning seasons out of nine and were 91-89, but won an RMC title in 1930–1931 and tied for another in 1936–1937. After Stegner left Utah, the Utes under Coach Peterson went on to win the NCAA Championship in 1944 and the National Invitational Tournament in 1947.

Certainly, the University of Utah in the 1920s and 1930s was not the flagship institution regionally and nationally that it now is, but like many small colleges and universities, then and now, it gave young people, often the first in their families to get an advanced education, an introduction to the world of ideas that would influence them for the rest of their lives.

Stegner remembered his university days in a variety of ways, but he also used three of his closest college friends for characters in one novel, *Recapitulation*. Jack Irvine, his tennis teammate, is undoubtedly the original for Joe Mulder of that novel. It was Robert Irvine, Jack's father, who gave the young Stegner a job as a salesman and deliveryman for his I&M Rug and Linoleum store at 251 South State. What Stegner says of the Mulder family's influence on Bruce Mason is true enough. When he goes to visit Joe Mulder (but leaves without ringing the door-bell), we read:

> If someone inside should turn on the light, the whole Mulder family would be caught, not like Jack Bailey, *in flagrante delicto,* but in their goodness and friendliness and warmth, their St. Bernard size and companionable numbers, their profound unanxious solidarity and confidence.... Jack Mormons, the Mulders did not tithe or go to meeting, but they kept the strenuous Mormon sense of stewardship. Having talents, one improved them. Having money or position, one tried to use it for the public good.[16]

Throughout *Recapitulation* Joe Mulder is a steadying and unfailing friend of Bruce, teaching him how to play tennis and serving as his constant companion. Jack Irvine, whose given name was Garner Davis Irvine, later became one of Utah's best-known antique dealers, died in 1987, and is buried at Wasatch Lawn Cemetery in Salt Lake City.

Mulder is not as important a character in *Recapitulation* as Bruce Mason's girlfriend, Nola, who in real life was Juanita Crawford, to whom Stegner was engaged. Juanita was born in Emery County on March 16, 1905; married another of Stegner's college friends, Marvin Broberg, after her engagement to Stegner was broken off; taught school in Salt Lake City; and died on September 9, 1974. With her husband and her son she is buried in the Salt Lake City Cemetery. Her daughter, Anne Broberg Riordan, is professor emeritus of modern dance at the University of Utah.

At one point in *Recapitulation* Bruce recalls after many years her beauty the night they went to a college dance at the Hotel Utah: "Nola in a party dress of green taffeta, her hair piled rich and dark on her head, his orchid pinned to her waist.... Her shoulders, rising bare out of the stiff green silk, are smooth and golden. She is as full of promise as the spring night outside." He remembers that "her dark piled hair among the shingle bobs and fresh marcels makes her seem more womanly than any girl in the room. She is not made for acrobatics or showing off; she is made for waltzes, slow fox-trots, circlings in uncrowded corners, long looks, murmured talk, serious questions, sober moments, upward smiles, communion. Her voice is husky, her laugh so warm and low that it makes the laughter of other girls sound like the cackling of hens." And he recalls them as a couple at the dance: "On the merest glance, he is younger than she—younger in years, younger in manners and self-command. He is blond where she is dark, his eyes are blue, where hers are brown, he is thin and hyperactive by contrast with her composure, darkly tanned where she is golden. She makes a center, he orbits it. She smiles, he laughs. He talks with his mouth, eyes, hands, body; she listens."[17]

In contrast to Nola is Holly, who in real life was Helen "Peg" Foster, a young woman born in southern Utah who married the famed journalist and expert on Chinese communism Edgar Snow in 1932 after she arrived in China and published a number of significant books (*My China Years; Inside Red China; The Chinese Communists,* in two volumes; and *Red Dust*) under the pen name Nym Wales. She and Edgar were divorced in 1949 (he then married Lois Wheeler, a prominent actress, who began her career with a supporting role in the premiere production of Arthur Miller's *All My Sons*). Foster died on January 11, 1997, at the age of eighty-nine and is buried in Connecticut. Her papers are in the Harold B. Lee Library at Brigham Young University.

In *Recapitulation* Bruce Mason is attracted to Holly as much as he is to Nola, but the two women are studies in contrast. As Bruce gets ready to go to the mortuary to make arrangements for the funeral of his aunt, he recalls the rooming house with the tower in which Holly lived during his undergraduate years, and the memories of Holly and her friends come rushing back:

That tower! With all the Jazz Age bohemians crawling in and out. Have-lock Ellis, Freud, Mencken, *The Memoirs of Fanny Hill, Love's Coming of Age, The Well of Loneliness,* Harry Kemp, Frank Harris. My Lord.

He was flooded with delighted recollection. They were all there before him—reed-necked aesthetes, provincial cognoscenti, sad sexy yokels, lovers burning with a hard, gem-like flame, a homosexual or two trying to look blasted and corroded by secret sin. Painters of bile-green landscapes, cubist photographers, poets, and iconoclasts, resident Dadaists, scorners of the bourgeoisie, makers of cherished prose, dream-tellers, correspondence-school psychoanalysts, they swarmed through Holly's apartment and eddied around her queenly shape with noises like breaking china. He remembered her in a gold gown, a Proserpine or a Circe. For an instant she was slim and tall in his mind and he saw her laughing in the midst of the excitement she created, and how her hair was smooth black and her eyes very dark blue and how she wore massive gold hoops in her ears.[18]

In an extended passage in *Recapitulation* Bruce compares the two women and his relationships with them: "Holly had scared him off because she took the offensive. She grabbed. He was too young and green, his bones hadn't hardened. By the time he had come to Nola, only weeks later, he was farther along. And Nola was a different girl, altogether other." Nola, he says, was put to sleep by art and books, but she had a wonderful musical talent: "How did a girl from a cow town on the edge of the slick rock country, ... how did such a girl from a starving and primitive little town get born with perfect pitch and the ability to play almost any instrument, after a try or two, by ear? Where did she learn so well to sing parts in her husky contralto? ... Singing, she was a warm and happy energy. Joy came out of her mouth." As Bruce remembers, "Where Holly was all vivacity, Nola was all repose.... There were head people and body people. Holly, for all her calculated glamour, lived above the neck. Nola, with no intentional glamour at all, lived below it." When Bruce tells Holly that he is in love with Nola, she says he's joking "in her light, high voice. A vanilla voice. Nola's was caramel, or chocolate."[19]

Bruce loses both Holly and Nola, and it is apparent as *Recapitulation* moves on that the two women are, with his mother, his brother, Joe Mulder, Jack Bailey, and Bill Bennion, part of the past he thought he had left behind before his return to Salt Lake City.

Several other characters in *Recapitulation* may come from Stegner's experiences at the university. Bill Bennion, the faculty member from the English Department who is so influential in Bruce Mason's undergraduate years, might be Sydney Angleman, who remained Stegner's close friend and correspondent until his death during open-heart surgery in the spring of 1971. Or it might be L. A. Quivey, for whom Stegner read student papers, as he also did for Angleman. Or Bennion might be a composite. The description of Bennion's office would hardly fit that of Angleman's (as this colleague knew it):

> The desk overflows with bluebooks and themes, the chairs are piled with books recently returned by undergraduate borrowers and not yet restored to the shelves, which anyway are too jammed with other books, cardboard boxes of notes, stacked magazines and wadded lunch bags smelling of banana skins to hold them. The wastebasket has overflowed onto the floor. On the window ledges and on the tops of the radiators the dust is thick over piles of mimeographed sheets that have been there in that condition ever since Bruce first came into the office as a sophomore.[20]

Perhaps Bennion is based on Angleman with Stegner's additions to make the character more colorful, or perhaps Bennion is an amalgam of several professors at the university.

Ham Barrentine, the tennis coach, might well be derived from Theron Parmelee, the legendary Ute tennis coach: "He goes up to Ham Barrentine's office and picks up his last [letter] sweater. Ham gets a little sentimental over the last four years and shakes his hand and grips his shoulder."[21]

The possible identity of one other character remains highly uncertain. Jack Bailey is the lecherous friend of Bruce and Joe, a young man smartly dressed who alternately fascinates and appalls his two friends with tales of his sexual conquests, both real and imagined. He is a failed Mormon missionary, having been sent home for sexual misbehavior. Several people familiar with Stegner's undergraduate circle of friends have suggested possible models for Bailey, but his real-life identity is probably better left alone.

One very minor character who may have had a real-life counterpart is Eddie Forsberg, a West Point cadet who returns to Salt Lake City to visit Nola and is both surprised and angry to find that she has given his West Point class ring to Bruce Mason. Forsberg may have been Bruce Easley, a young man Juanita Crawford went steady with during her high school years in Ferron, Utah.

Stegner, however, would remind us, as he said to Richard Etulain, the prominent western historian, in *Conversations with Wallace Stegner on Western History and Literature,* "Fiction demands some changes in a character in order to make him fictionally persuasive and coherent." Or, as Stegner told James Hepworth, when asked why readers often fail to distinguish between author and narrator: "What does Wallace Stegner have to do with it? The very fact that some of my experience goes into the book is all but inescapable, and true for almost any writer I can name. Which is real and which is invented is (a) nobody's business and (b) a rather silly preoccupation and (c) impossible to answer. By the time I'm through converting my life into fiction it's half fiction at least and maybe more."[22]

Stegner's seven years at the University of Utah were far more influential than he realized at the time. His friends, his professors, the library, and the academic ambience all gave him memories and intellectual riches that helped to make him the distinguished writer and humanitarian he became. As he says at the end of his essay on his university years:

It is ultimately the love of books that I owe them. As an organism, I have outlived nearly all those who taught me most, but their influence still works in me, and I am still grateful for the warmth and openness of their friendship. As my tennis-and-basketball-playing friends ushered me into the human world and taught me how to belong, this handful of teacher-friends introduced me to the life of the mind where, even though I didn't know it then, I most wanted to live. No university, even the greatest, could have done much more.[23]

Coming from an unstable home, having to struggle with his self-image, and finding his way to intellectual maturity at the university, Stegner was ready to move on to one of the most distinguished American literary careers of the twentieth century.

PART II

✦ *Wallace Stegner on Salt Lake City* ✦

At Home in the Fields of the Lord

Wallace Stegner

I HAVE ALWAYS ENVIED PEOPLE with a hometown. They always seem to have an attic, and in the attic albums of pictures, spellers used in the third grade, gocarts and Irish mails with the scars of young heels and teeth on them. In the houses of these fortunate ones there is always some casual friend of thirty or forty years' standing, someone who grew up next door, some childhood sweetheart, some inseparable companion from primary days. Some people even live in the houses their fathers and grandfathers used; and no matter how wide they may scatter from the hometown, always behind them is a solid backstop of cousins and grandmothers and relatives once or twice removed, maintaining the solidarity and permanence of the clan.

None of these forms of moss clings to a rolling stone, and I was born rolling. If I met a playmate of forty years ago we would not recognize each other even as names. Since I left them (or they me) to move elsewhere, I have never again encountered a single one of the children I knew in any of my various dwelling places. The things that accumulate in others' attics and in their memories, to turn up again in their futures, have been cleaned out of mine five dozen times to simplify moves. Since I was born in Iowa in 1909 (my hometown held me six weeks) I have lived in twenty places in eight different states, besides a couple of places in Canada, and in some of these places we lived in anywhere from two to ten different houses and neighborhoods. This is not quite the same thing as traveling extensively; it involves having no permanent base whatever. Until my wife and I built a house I am sure no member of my family had ever owned one.

The absence of roots has always seemed to me a deprivation both person-ally and professionally. Personally, I was condemned to friendships that were always being sharply cut off and rarely renewed, so that for a time they tried to live by mail and then lamely dwindled out. Professionally, as a writer, I considered myself unequipped with the enduring relationships from which the deepest understand-ing of people might have come. I have always thought of myself as a sort of social and literary air plant, without the sustaining roots that luckier people have. And I am always embarrassed when well-meaning people ask where I am from.

That is why I have been astonished, on a couple of recent trips through Salt Lake City, to find a conviction growing in me that I am not as homeless as I had thought. At worst, I had thought myself an Ishmael; at best, a half stranger in the city where I had lived the longest, a Gentile in the New Jerusalem. But a dozen years of absence from Zion, broken only by two or three short revisitings, have taught me different. I am as rich in a hometown as anyone, though I adopted my home as an adolescent and abandoned it as a young man.

A Gentile in the New Jerusalem: certainly I was. Salt Lake City is a divi-ded concept, a complex idea. To the devout it is more than a place; it is a way of life, a corner of the materially realizable heaven; its soil is held together by the roots of the family and the cornerstones of the temple. In this sense Salt Lake City is forever foreign to me, as to any non-Mormon. But in spite of being a Gentile I discover that much of my youth is there, and a surprising lot of my heart. Having blown tumbleweed-fashion around the continent so that I am forced to *select* a hometown, I find myself selecting the City of the Saints, and for what seems to me cause.

It has such a comfortable, old-clothes feel that it is a shock to see again how beautiful this town really is, quite as beautiful as the Chamber of Commerce says it is; how it lies under a bright clarity of light and how its outlines are clean and spacious, how it is dignified with monuments and steeped in sun tempered with shade, and how it lies protected behind its rampart mountains, insulated from the stormy physical and intellectual weather of both coasts. Serenely concerned with itself, it is probably open to criticism as an ostrich city; its serenity may be possible only in a fool's paradise of isolationism and provincialism and smugness. But what is a hometown if it is not a place you feel secure in? I feel secure in Salt Lake City, and I know why. Because I keep meeting so many things I know, so many things that have not changed since I first saw the city in 1921.

True, it has grown by at least fifty thousand people since then, new roads have been built and new industries imported, new streets of houses are strung out from the old city limits. But there were people and roads and industries and houses there before; these new ones have not changed the town too much, and seem hardly to have affected its essential feel at all.

It was an amazement to me, returning, to realize how much I know about this city until I remembered that I had lived there off and on for nearly fifteen years; that as a Boy Scout I had made an elaborate and detailed map of its streets in order to pass some test or other; that as a high school student I had solicited advertisements among all its business houses; that while I was in college I had worked afternoons in a store that was always in need of somebody to double as a truck driver, so that I delivered parcels lengthwise and endwise over the city. There is no better way to learn a place; I have known no place in that way since.

Moreover, Salt Lake is an easy town to know. You can see it all. Lying in a great bowl valley, it can be surmounted and comprehended and possessed wholly as few cities can. You can't possibly get lost in it. The Wasatch comes with such noble certitude up from the south and curves so snugly around the "Avenues" that from anywhere in the city you can get your directions and find your way. And man has collaborated with Nature to make sure that you can't get lost. The streets are marked by a system so logical that you can instantly tell not merely where you are but exactly how far you are from anywhere else. And when your mind contains, as

I found recently that mine did, not merely this broad plat but a great many of the little lost half streets with names like Elm and Barbara and Pierpont, then you have blocked off one of the great sources of nightmare.

You can't get lost. That is much. And you can always see where you are. That is even more. And you can get clear up above the city and look all the way around and over it, and that is most. Looking into the blank walls of cities or staring up at them from dirty canyon sidewalks breeds things in people that eventually have to be lanced.

Sure and comfortable knowledge is reinforced by association, which often amounts to love and always involves some emotional relationship. Mere familiarity, I suppose, generates an emotional attachment of a kind, but when years of the most emotionally active time of one's life have been spent among certain streets and houses and schools and people and countrysides, the associational emotion is so pervasive that it may be entirely overlooked for years, and comprehended only in retrospect. Nostalgia, the recognition of old familiarity, is the surest way to recognize a hometown.

In a way, my family's very mobility helped to make this town peculiarly mine, for we lived in many neighborhoods. We lived at Fifth South and Fifth East under old cottonwoods behind a mangy lawn; we lived on Seventh East across from Liberty Park so that I knew intimately the rats in the open surplus canal; we lived in a bungalow on Eighth East, an old brick ruin on Twenty-first South and State, a pleasant house on Fifteenth East above the high school I attended. We lived on Ninth East and Fourth South, on Seventh South and Eleventh East, in an apartment on First Avenue, in an ancient adobe down near the heart of town by the post office. I beat my way to school across lots from many different directions, and my memory is tangled in the trees on certain old streets and involved in the paths across many vacant lots and impromptu baseball fields.

The mere act of writing them down amplifies and extends the things that remain with me from having lived deeply and widely in Salt Lake City. I suppose I played tennis on almost every public and private court in town, and I know I hiked over every golf course. For three or four winters, with a club basketball team, I ran myself ragged in the frigid amusement halls of a hundred Mormon ward houses and took icy showers and went home blown and rubber-legged late at night. With a team in the commercial league, or with the freshman squad at the university, I hit all the high school gyms, as well as the old rickety Deseret Gymnasium next door to the Utah Hotel, where cockroaches as big and dangerous as roller skates might be stepped on behind the dark lockers. From games and parties I ran home under dark trees, imagining myself as swift and tireless as Paavo Nurmi, and the smell and taste of that cold, smoky, autumnal air and the way the arc lights blurred in rounded golden blobs at the corners is with me yet. It makes those streets of twenty and twenty-five years ago as real as any I walk now; those are the streets I judge all other city streets by, and perhaps always will.

This, I discover belatedly, is the city of many firsts: the first car, the first dates, the first jobs. No moon has ever swum so beguilingly up over mountains as it used to swim up over the Wasatch; none has ever declined so serenely as it used to decline sometimes when we came home at two or three after a date and a twenty-mile drive out to Taylorsville or Riverton to take our girls home. No friends have ever so closely and effortlessly touched the heart. No sandwiches have ever since had the wonderful smoky flavor that the barbecued beef used to have at the old Night Owl on Ninth South, by the ball park. No heroes have ever walked so tall as Willie Kamm and Tony Lazzeri and Lefty O'Doul and Duffy Lewis and Paul Strand and Fritz Coumbe of the old Salt Lake Bees in the Pacific Coast League. The year Tony Lazzeri hit sixty home runs over the short left field fence at Bonneville Park I haunted State Street, outside that fence, and risked death in traffic a hundred times to chase batting-practice balls and get a free seat in the left field bleachers. And when Coumbe, who had pitched (I believe) for the Athletics and played against Babe Ruth (Ruth hit the first ball he threw him over the centerfield fence) came to live in the other half of a duplex from us, and brought other heroes home with him, and gave me a left-handed first base mitt that had belonged to George Sisler, I grew twelve inches overnight.

Here for the first time I can remember triumphs, or what seemed triumphs then. In Salt Lake I wrote my first short story and my first novel. In Salt Lake I fell in love for the first time and was rudely jilted for the first time and recovered for the first time. In Salt Lake I took my first drink and acquired a delightful familiarity with certain speakeasies that I could find now blindfold if there were any necessity. I experimented with ether beer and peach brandy and bathtub gin and survived them all, as I survived the experience of driving an automobile at sixteen or seventeen, by hairbreadth but satisfactory margins.

It seems to me now that in the course of one activity or another, driven by that furious and incomprehensible adolescent energy which lies dead somewhere in Salt Lake and which I wish I could bring back as readily as I bring back its memory, I surged up and down and across the New Jerusalem from Murray to Beck's Hot Springs, and from Saltair to Brighton and Pinecrest. And how it was, its weathers and its lights, is very clear to me.

So is the country that surrounds the city and that gives the city so much of its spaciousness and charm and a large part of its nostalgic tug.

Salt Lake lies in the lap of mountains. East of it, within easy reach of any boy, seven canyons lead directly up into another climate, to fishing and hunting and camping and climbing and winter skiing. Those canyons opened out of my back yard, no matter what house I happened to be living in. City Creek and Dry Canyon were immediate and walkable. Parley's could be penetrated by the judicious who hung around on the tracks behind the state penitentiary and hooked onto D&RG freights as they began to labor on the grade. Sometimes we rode a boxcar or a gondola; sometimes an indulgent fireman let us ride on the coal in the tender. Up in the canyon we could drop off anywhere, because even with two engines on, the train would only be going ten or fifteen miles an hour. South of Parley's was Mill Creek, and this we reached on more elaborate expeditions with knapsacks. In spring there were lucerne fields and orchards to go through toward the canyon's mouth, and the lucerne patches could always be counted on to provide a racer snake or two, and the orchards a pocketful of cherries or apricots. On a hot day, after a climb, cherries chilled in the cold water of Mill Creek and cherished, one by one, past teeth and palate and throat, were such cherries as the world has not produced since.

And the other canyons: the little swale of Hughes, where in late April the dogtooth violets were a blanket under the oakbrush; Big Cottonwood, up which ore trucks used to give us a lift to the Maxwell or the Cardiff mine, and where the peaks went in a granite whorl around the lakes and cottages of Brighton; Little Cottonwood, with the ghost town of Alta at its head, since famous for ski slopes; and Bell's, a glacial U with waterfalls and hanging glacial meadows lifting in a long steep southward curve toward Long Peak and the point of the mountain, from which we could look down on the narrows where the Jordan River slipped between alluvial gravel slopes toward the dead sea.

Knowing Salt Lake City means knowing its canyons, too, for no city of my acquaintance except possibly Reno breaks off so naturally and easily into fine free country. The line between city and mountains is as clean as the line between a port city and salt water. Up in the Wasatch is another world, distinct and yet contributory, and a Salt Lake boyhood is inevitably colored by it.

There is a limit to the indulgence of recollection, for fear nostalgia should be overcome by total recall. But it is clear to me, now that I have chosen a hometown, that I do not believe unqualifiedly in a "most impressionable age" between five and ten. The lag between experience and the kind of assimilation that can produce nostalgia is considerable, I suppose. In our early maturity we have just come to realize how much our tender minds absorbed in early childhood. But later we may have other realizations. Other recollections brighten as the first ones fade, and the recognition that now makes me all but skinless as I drive down Thirteenth East Street in Salt Lake City is every bit as sharp and indelible as the impressions my blank-page senses took as a child. Not all experience, not even all romantic and nostalgic experience, is equivalent to Wordsworth's.

Any place deeply lived in, any place where the vitality has been high and the emotions freely involved can fill the sensory attic with images enough for a lifetime of nostalgia. Because I believe in the influence of places on personalities, I think it somehow important that certain songs we sang as high school or college students in the twenties still mean particular and personal things. "I'm Looking over a Four Leaf Clover" is all tied up with the late-dusk smell of October on Second South and Twelfth East, and the shine of the arc light on the split street tipping up the Second South hill. "When Day Is Done" has the linseed oil smell of yellow slickers in it, and the feel of the soft corduroy cuffs those slickers had, and the colors of John Held pictures painted on the backs. "Exactly Like You" means the carpet, the mezzanine, the very look and texture and smell, of the Temple Square Hotel.

Salt Lake is not my hometown because my dead are buried there, or because I lived certain years of my youth and the first years of my marriage there, or because my son was born there. Duration alone does not do it. I have since spent half as many years in Cambridge, Massachusetts, without bringing from that residence more than a pitiful handful of associations. I was not living in Cambridge at the pace and with the complete uncritical participation that swept me along in Salt Lake. To recall anything about Cambridge is an effort, almost an act of will—though time may teach me I took more from there, too, than I thought I did. But Salt Lake City, revisited either in fact or in imagination, drowns me in acute recognitions, as if I had not merely sipped from but been doused with Proust's cup of reminding tea.

From its founding, Salt Lake City has been sanctuary: that has been its justification and its function. And it is as sanctuary that it persists even in my Gentile mind and insinuates itself as my veritable hometown. Yet there are darker and more ambiguous associations attached to it, and it is strange to me, returning, to find myself looking upon Salt Lake as the place of my security. It never was at the time I lived there. I suppose no age of a man is less secure than adolescence, and more subject to anguishes, and I think I do not exaggerate in believing that my own adolescence had most of the usual anguishes and some rather special ones besides. Certainly some of the years I lived in Salt Lake City were the most miserable years of my life, with their share of death and violence and more than their share of fear, and I am sure now that off and on and for considerable periods I can hardly have been completely sane.

There are houses and neighborhoods in Salt Lake whose associations are black and unhappy, places where we lived which I thought of at the time as prisons. Yet revisiting the city I am warmed by this flood of recollection, the unhappiness dwindles into proportion or perspective, even unimportance. Or perhaps the unhappiness takes on a glow in retrospect, and perhaps the feeling of security and well-being which Salt Lake gives me now is partly satisfaction at having survived here things that might have destroyed me. Or perhaps it arises from the pure brute satisfaction of having experienced anything, even misery, with that much depth and sharpness. Or perhaps, like the discomforts of a camping trip that become hilarious in the telling, the verbal formulation of distress has the capacity to cure it. So Emerson, after flunking a mathematics examination in college, could go home and triumph over all the arts of numbers by writing a destructive essay on the subject.

I suppose that may come close to the core of my feeling about Salt Lake. Returning is a satisfactory literary experience; the present has power to evoke a more orderly version of the past. And what is evoked, though it may be made of unpleasant or unhappy elements, is satisfactory because it *is* a kind of vicarious thing, a literary product.

Whether it says with the Anglo-Saxon poet, "That have I borne, this can I bear also," or whether it says, "There, for a while, I lived life to the hilt, and so let come what may," my hometown, late discovered, is not a deprivation or a loss or a yearning backward. I recently had the experience of recognizing, and with pleasure, what the city meant to me, but I was not heartbroken to leave either it or that youth of mine that it embalms, and I do not necessarily yearn to return to either. It does not destroy me with a sense of lost green childhood or of any intimation of immortality long gone and irrecoverable. There is only this solid sense of having had or having been or having lived something real and good and satisfying, and the knowledge that having had or been or lived these things I can never lose them again. Home is what you can take away with you.

It Is the Love of Books I Owe Them

WALLACE STEGNER

I AM COMING ALONG THIRTEENTH EAST on my way to an eight o'clock class. It is a marvelous morning—it is always a marvelous morning, whether the air is hazy with autumn and the oakbrush on the Wasatch has gone bronze and gold, or whether the chestnut trees along the street are coned with blossoms. The early sun slants across lawns and throws tree-shadows halfway across the pavement and warms the faces of houses on the other side. Cars pass, people wave, walkers across the street give me greeting—faces that I am glad to see, and that are glad to see me. I am enveloped in universal friendliness. As I turn at the drugstore on Second South and start uphill toward the Park Building at the head of the U drive, I meet Harold, the enthusiastic imbecile who appoints himself cheerleader at all athletic events and wants to be mascot to everybody in the college. Harold wears a leather jacket, he has wild hair and windmill arms, he bursts with more ardor than his wild arms and his clogged voice can express. His affection is as wriggling and ingratiating as a puppy's. Often he watches tennis matches, and he knows me as a hero. We slap each other on the back and exchange pleasantries. His sweet adoring smile hangs on the morning air of the dream, welcoming me into a day placid and without threat and rich with possibility, and then I pass and he fades like breath off a mirror, leaving only his warmth behind.

Why that recurrent dream? Whence all that sweetness and light and trust and sense of well-being? It is notorious that memory, like a sundial, wants to count no hours but the sunny ones; but dreams, which use memory for other purposes, including punishment, are another matter. Put your arm into those dark waters and you are likely to find them writhing with snakes, or transformed by guilt into a pool of excrement. School dreams especially are often haunted by anxiety, dread of failure, and the conviction of inadequacy. When I dream of East High School I am usually being humiliated, or I am fleeing somebody or something up and down mazes of corridors, flights of wide steps, narrow passages so tight they squeeze the soul. Or I have registered for a course and incomprehensibly forgotten all about it. Now suddenly I realize I must take an exam in it, and I have never attended a class or cracked a book. I don't even know the name of the course or the teacher. In panic I run down those corridors opening doors, hoping for some clue, something familiar. Only the bent backs of strangers busily writing, and the disapproving eyes of a teacher wondering what I want and why I interrupt people like this. The clock in the corridor tells a dreadful story of time rushing by, opportunity vanishing. The principal collars me, asking why I am not at my exam? In blind panic I stammer, trying to explain, but I grow garbled and incoherent under his glare, and end by waking myself with my own animal sounds.

About the University of Utah I do not dream that way. Instead, over and over, I dream some variant of that sunny morning on the way to class, in a world full of friends including Harold, Old Innocence himself, who greets me with joy, looking out of the corners of his eyes at passersby to make sure they have seen him in friendly conversation with a college man.

I know why that difference. Despite some things that, too well remembered, might persuade me otherwise, I think those years between 1925 and 1930 when I was an undergraduate at the University of Utah were the happiest time of my life—certainly the happiest up to that point. Not even the censorious desk sergeant who books my dreams can distort the pleasant images I retain. I came as a scared sixteen-year-old freshman into an expanding universe, and for a while expanded with it.

Simply growing up was part of it. When I graduated from East High I was physically a runt, as much a mascot as Harold. People kidded me, and condescended to me, but nobody could conceivably have been my *friend*. Then all at once I grew six inches, and was on the human scale. It didn't matter that at six feet and 125 pounds I was probably the skinniest kid in the college. That could be taken care of. I spent every free hour in the gym wearing out the weight machines and running laps. I went out for basketball and then for tennis. One of the most blindingly satisfying moments of my freshman year came when Stan Rock, the fullback who handed out towels in the cage, looked at me with respect and remarked that here was the kid who worked out more than anybody in school.

Another such moment came when I made the tennis team and acquired a letter sweater to drape over my bones like a rag over a gate. It was that sweater that made Harold look on me as one of the godlike ones who belonged. To tell the truth, it had the same effect on me.

Along with growth, friends. There have been no such friends since. If they were more athletes than scholars, I needn't apologize for them. They were hearts of gold, and they accepted *me*. Tennis players such as Jack Irvine, Chick Blevins, Lin Crone, Mel Gallagher, Dave Freed, and Met Wilson; the Tillicums Club that played as a basketball team in intramural tournaments, the city industrial league, and dozens of Ward House amusement halls; runners like Red Cowan, all-arounders like Jim Gilbert, football players like Ray Forsberg and Ted Aldous and LeGrand Dyckman and Baldy Simpkins, crewcut and extroverted basketball players like Hap Libbert—they made an environment in which I was as happy as a shrimp in cocktail sauce. The life of the mind came off a distant second.

For a while during my inevitable sophomore slump, the life of the mind looked as if it might drop out of the race altogether. Moreover, from the spring of my freshman year onward it had, in addition to all the sports, friends, girls, parties, and fraternity activities, the stiff competition of an outside job. Through most of four years I concentrated all my classes in the mornings and worked from one to six on weekdays and eight to six on Saturdays at the I&M Rug and Linoleum Company, owned by Jack Irvine's father. And not content with squeezing the intellectual life into so narrow a space, I was also playing varsity tennis every spring, editing the *Pen,* and reading papers for Sydney Angleman, L. A. Quivey, or Edward Chapman, or all three at once. I remember a spell of six whole months when I did all my studying between midnight and three in the morning. Most of those four years I was in love with somebody or other, and girls in the twenties were great time-eaters. For the last year and a half of my college life I had stomach ulcers. Altogether, if I had deliberately set out to expose myself as little as possible to an education, I could hardly have arranged a better program.

Perhaps the University did not demand enough. In those years it was not the great and growing institution it now is. Physically it was hardly more than a cluster of old buildings around the horseshoe drive. There was no auditorium, no Marriott Library, no Student Union, no medical school, no field house, no stadium.

The library was small, not well stocked, not well used. The faculty was less than world famous. The three or four thousand students mainly lived at home and came to school on the streetcar. In that time before the Great Depression, before World War II, before Korea and Vietnam, this provincial institution slept behind its protecting mountains and only a little of the turbulence of the twenties got through. Bobbed hair, short skirts, rolled stockings, yes; intellectual unrest, not so clearly. From here, it all looks like the age of innocence.

And yet, for all its easy-going atmosphere, and despite all my apparent effort to avoid contamination by ideas, the University did reach me. It reached me early and it continued to reach me, often when I didn't know it was doing so. Although by investing my time in other things, particularly in more hours of outside work than I should have been permitted, I left holes in my education that now will never be filled, I did absorb something of what I was offered. From the first day of classes, I met teachers who influenced and excited me. World famous most of them were not, or ever became so. But they were teachers, and they taught in a friendly environment. Many of them were still there to become my colleagues when I returned to Utah to teach after some years in graduate school. Some of them are still there, and still among my closest friends, after nearly half a century. Because of their affiliation with the university, they have stayed put, and been more persistently accessible than the people who were my fellow students.

The fact is, some of them were my close friends even when I was a student. They gave me, in and out of the classroom, what I seemed so hell-bent to avoid.

For instance, Vardis Fisher, my freshman English instructor, announced on the first day that he intended to take a can-opener to our closed minds. He sounded a note of intellectual recklessness that contradicted the complacency of the campus. I worked like a slave for him, and before long was a member of the so-called Radical Club that he and Don Lewis, an instructor in speech, had formed. Our radicalism was pretty innocent. Meeting generally at Fisher's apartment, we listened to a paper on the historicity of Jesus Christ (Vardis was of the opinion that he was probably ahistorical), or discussed Margaret Sanger and birth control, or sat in a mute admiring circle to listen to Scott Nearing, who had recently been dismissed from (I think) the University of Pennsylvania for his dangerous ideas. Isolated, far-off, adrift among our native deserts and mountains, we heard echoes of intransigence and change and were led to books that in class we could have discussed only gingerly, if at all. It seems to me we were radical mainly in relation to sex. I remember reading Havelock Ellis, Freud, Edward Carpenter's *Love's Coming of Age,* but I can't remember ever reading Marx or Engels or anybody political in that company.

The Radical Club, and indeed the whole area of books and ideas, was a separate part of my expanding universe. It led me toward a quite different set of associates. Looking backward, I discover that very few of the friends with whom I was closest were much interested in books and ideas, and that very few of the students who *were* interested in them were people I liked extremely. That may be symptomatic of a general anti-intellectualism in my time and my crowd; it may only have been a piece of bad luck. Or maybe it was good luck, for it did throw me, for the satisfaction of those hungers which I had barely begun to recognize, into the company of faculty members. More out of class than in, they gave my quite unfurnished mind whatever decoration it got, and as decorators they were undoubtedly sounder, and certainly less faddish, than any of my peers would have been.

They were only a handful, and almost all in the English department, but I owe them an inordinate amount. Fisher, who was not exactly lovable but was anything but dull, stayed only a year or two and was gone. Before he left he not only had pried open my closed skull but had planted within it an ambition to write. He excused me from the last two quarters of freshman English and enlisted me in an advanced writing course. A year or so later I was led to L. A. Quivey's course in creative writing, where I tried to write short stories. Mr. Quivey was not a writer himself, but he knew approximately ten thousand times more about writing than I did, and he made me learn a great deal. He was also unfailingly kind and encouraging. By the time I was a junior I was reading papers for him: one of the quaint informalities of that time before the development of a graduate school was that a student considered "bright" by his instructor might be put to judging his contemporaries.

Mr. Quivey was related to Scott Fitzgerald, or perhaps Zelda Fitzgerald. Or perhaps he only knew somebody who was related to one or the other. Or perhaps he only fantasized some relationship. In any case he radiated an enthusiasm for Fitzgerald's writing that I tried, not always successfully, to share. Other enthusiasms from other sources I had less difficulty with. Two young instructors, Sydney Angleman and Edward Chapman, opened themselves and their offices to me; I spent as much time there as I did in the gym, probably, and at that time when everything else in my life was leading me away from books, they made me, and kept me, a reader. God knows when I found time to read, but I did—on the streetcar, I suppose. Inevitably I missed many things. Sometimes whole authors eluded me, as T. S. Eliot did. When Joe Hanson, one of Quivey's favorites who was many years later Leon Trotsky's secretary in Mexico, rose up in Keeley's ice cream parlor after a movie, and, gravely drunk, announced that all life boiled down to "birth, copulation, death," I was envious. I wished I had said that. I thought he had made it up. But on other writers I would have been more knowing. I read Anderson, Hemingway, Fitzgerald, Willa Cather, Frost, Yeats, the Imagists. I wandered into Anatole France and Knut Hamsun. I was letter-perfect on some writers who were big in the twenties and later shrank—Joseph Hergesheimer and James Branch Cabell for two. I borrowed Syd Angleman's smuggled copy of *Ulysses* and sat up all night with it and went off dazedly to my eight o'clock class with the volume clutched in my hand and my brains dizzy with words. I was, in short, a pretty literary young man without particularly realizing it. If my girl friend of the moment would hold still for it, I was as likely to quote her lines from Blake as to tell her what she wanted to hear.

Most of this was extracurricular and supplementary, but classes too confirmed me in my literary stance. They gave me, as I discovered when I went away to graduate school, a reasonably solid grounding in English and American literature. I am grateful that what they taught was primarily the books themselves, not glosses and critical commentary on the books. Sherman Brown Neff, who during most of my time at Utah was head of the English department, had a rather old-fashioned way of teaching poetry: he read it aloud. The result, for me, was that he filled my head with stanzas and lines and passages. Like Syd Angleman and Edward Chapman, he was a lover of what he taught, not one of that more recent tribe who infest the English departments and do their best to make students feel superior to what they read.

It is ultimately the love of books that I owe them. As an organism, I have outlived nearly all those who taught me most, but their influence still works in me, and I am still grateful for the warmth and openness of their friendship. As my tennis-and-basketball-playing friends ushered me into the human world and taught me how to belong, this handful of teacher-friends introduced me to the life of the mind where, even though I didn't know it then, I most wanted to live. No university, even the greatest, could have done much more.

PART III

Photo Essay

East High School, 1300 East and 900 South, from which Wallace and Cecil Stegner graduated in 1925. The original building was replaced with a seismic-resistant building in the late twentieth century.

Wallace Stegner (*left*), senior picture, East High School (East High School *Eastonia*, 1925). Cecil Stegner (*right*), senior picture, East High School (East High School *Eastonia*, 1925).

Wallace Stegner and Juanita Crawford at Fish Lake, ca. 1927.

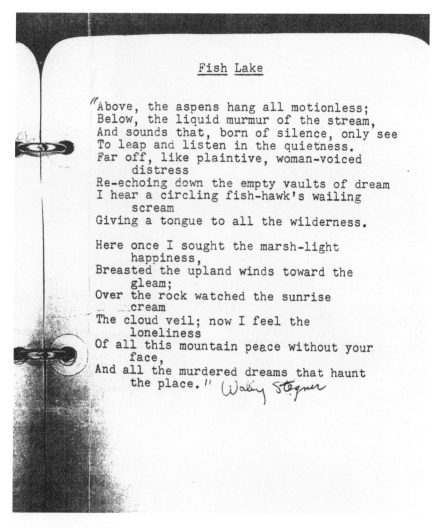

Fish Lake

"Above, the aspens hang all motionless;
Below, the liquid murmur of the stream,
And sounds that, born of silence, only see
To leap and listen in the quietness.
Far off, like plaintive, woman-voiced
        distress
Re-echoing down the empty vaults of dream
I hear a circling fish-hawk's wailing
        scream
Giving a tongue to all the wilderness.

Here once I sought the marsh-light
        happiness,
Breasted the upland winds toward the
        gleam;
Over the rock watched the sunrise
        cream
The cloud veil; now I feel the
        loneliness
Of all this mountain peace without your
        face,
And all the murdered dreams that haunt
        the place." Wally Stegner

Poem written by Wallace Stegner to Juanita Crawford, ca. 1930.

Juanita Crawford, the original for the character Nola Gordon in *Recapitulation.* "Her voice is husky, her laugh so warm and low that it makes the laughter of other girls sound like the cackling of hens.... How did a girl ... from a starving and primitive little town get born with perfect pitch and the ability to play almost any instrument, after a try or two, by ear? Where did she learn so well to sing parts in her husky contralto?... Singing, she was a warm and happy energy. Joy came out of her mouth" (*Recapitulation*, 63, 132).

Helen "Peg" Foster, the original for the character Holly in *Recapitulation.* "He remembered her in a gold gown, a Proserpine or a Circe. For an instant she was slim and tall in his mind and he saw her laughing in the midst of the excitement she created" (*Recapitulation,* 5).

Jack Irvine (*left*), Scott Miller (*in water*), and Wallace Stegner (*right*) in a Wasatch Mountains canyon, late 1920s. Irvine and Stegner were close friends and varsity tennis teammates at the University of Utah. The Irvine and Miller families owned the I&M Rug and Linoleum Company at which Stegner worked during his college years.

Wallace Stegner at Fish Lake in southern
Utah, where the Stegner family had a cabin,
ca. late 1920s.

IRVINE
STEGNER
Captain

Jack Irvine (*left*) and Wallace Stegner, University of Utah varsity tennis team, ca. late 1920s. Jack Irvine is the original for Joe Mulder in *The Big Rock Candy Mountain* and *Recapitulation.*

Mary and Wallace Stegner, at or
shortly after their wedding, 1934.

Vardis Fisher, professor of English at the University of Utah. He later became Idaho's best-known writer. "Vardis Fisher, my freshman English instructor, announced on the first day that he intended to take a can-opener to our closed minds. He sounded a note of intellectual recklessness that contradicted the complacency of the campus. I worked like a slave for him" ("It Is the Love of Books I Owe Them," 116).

Sydney Angleman, English Department, University of Utah. Angleman served as dean, vice president, and departmental chair. He was known as "the conscience of the university." "And not content with squeezing the intellectual life into so narrow a space, I was also playing varsity tennis every spring, editing the *Pen,* and reading papers for Sydney Angleman, L. A. Quivey, or Edward Chapman, or all three at once. I remember a spell of six whole months when I did all my studying between midnight and three in the morning" ("It Is the Love of Books I Owe Them," 114).

Edward Chapman, English Department, University of Utah.

Sherman Neff, English Department, University of Utah. "Sherman Brown Neff, who during most of my time at Utah was head of the English department, had a rather old-fashioned way of teaching poetry: he read it aloud. The result, for me, was that he filled my head with stanzas and lines and passages. Like Syd Angleman and Edward Chapman, he was a lover of what he taught, not one of that more recent tribe who infest the English departments and do their best to make students feel superior to what they read" ("It Is the Love of Books I Owe Them," 120).

FORSBERG   IRVINE   STEGNER   FREED   SMITH

University of Utah varsity tennis team, 1929. *Left to right:* Ray Forsberg, Jack Irvine, Wallace Stegner, David Freed, Harold Smith (1929 *Utonian*).

Stegner   Grover   Thomas   Rasmussen   Hall
     Brown   Nicholson   Thatcher   Winn

Wallace Stegner (*upper left*) as president of Sigma Epsilon, an honorary literary fraternity (1931 *Utonian*).

Hilda Emilia Stegner's grave marker in the Salt Lake City Cemetery in the Park section, plot 37-6-4W. She is the Ella Mason of *The Big Rock Candy Mountain* and *Recapitulation.*

Cecil Lawrence Stegner's grave marker in the Salt Lake City Cemetery in the Park section, plot 37-6-5W. He is the Chet Mason of *The Big Rock Candy Mountain* and *Recapitulation.*

Tony Lazzeri of the Salt Lake Bees set the long-standing minor-league record for home runs for one season with 60 in 1925. "The year Tony Lazzeri hit sixty home runs over the short left field fence at Bonneville Park I haunted State Street, outside that fence, and risked death in traffic a hundred times to chase batting-practice balls and get a free seat in the left field bleachers" ("At Home in the Fields of the Lord," 163).

Wallace Stegner, ASUU student card,
winter quarter, 1930.

Sigma Nu fraternity house, 1246 East Second South, Stegner's fraternity
(1930 *Utonian*). It is now a private residence.

University of Utah, 1925, founded in 1850 as the University
of Deseret. It was moved to its present location in 1896. Fort
Douglas is in the background to the east.

University of Utah, ca. 1920s. Panorama of the University of Utah
looking southeast to the Wasatch Range.

Cummings Field (*above*),
used until 1927 and then
replaced by Ute Stadium.

Ute Stadium (*right*),
(later Rice Stadium),
used until 1998 and then
replaced by Rice-Eccles
Stadium.

Whitewashing the U (*right*), located east of the university, ca. 1920s. The whitewashing was annually performed by the students. The old U was replaced by a new one with erosion control and variable colored lighting in 2005.

Students by the John R. Park Building (*below*), which now houses the university administration, ca. 1920s.

Keeley's Candy and Ice Cream Store, 55 South Main Street, 1917. Neither the business nor the building still exist. "When Joe Hanson ... rose up in Keeley's ice cream parlor after a movie, and, gravely drunk, announced that all life boiled down to 'birth, copulation, death,' I was envious. I wished I had said that" ("It Is the Love of Books I Owe Them," 119).

First Stegner home, 1191 South 700 East, summer 1921. "Coming in along Seventh South [*sic*] along Liberty Park, he drove slowly, looking for the first house they had lived in in Salt Lake, the one with the bullet hole beside the door. He recognized nothing" (*Recapitulation*, 242). Liberty Park actually lies between 700 East and 500 East and between 900 South and 1300 South. At another point in *Recapitulation*, Stegner correctly locates the home "on Seventh East, across from Liberty Park" (31).

Deseret Gymnasium, located across the street to the east from Temple Square in the Joseph Smith Memorial Building block. It was a public gymnasium built and operated by the LDS Church. The building is no longer extant. "With a team in the commercial league, or with the freshman squad at the university, I hit all the high school gyms, as well as the old rickety Deseret Gymnasium next door to the Utah Hotel, where cockroaches as big and dangerous as roller skates might be stepped on behind the dark lockers" ("At Home in the Fields of the Lord," 162).

Salt Lake Public Library, on the east side of State Street between South Temple Street and 100 South Street, ca. 1920s. It later housed the Hansen Planetarium but is currently vacant. "I found the public library. I didn't really find it until we got to Salt Lake, but I lived in it in Salt Lake. Books are a habit, and once you've created a book-habit, I suppose it lasts" (Stegner and Etulain, *Conversations with Stegner,* 51).

Warm Springs, a public swimming pool and recreation
facility. The business no longer exists, and the building
is vacant. [Elsa to Bruce:] "Maybe you could go swimming." "Where? There's only Warm Springs, and last time
I was out there I got a bealed ear" (*Recapitulation*, 96).

Salt Lake Tennis Club (*above*), 1000 East between 200 South and 300 South. The site is now occupied by a senior-citizens center. Bruce Mason sees "two girls playing on the first court. They banged the ball ferociously, they ran like sprinters, they slid and changed directions and charged up and fell back, they chopped and lobbed and drove and smashed and volleyed in grim, breathless competitiveness, they chased each other from corner to corner and from net to base line" (*Recapitulation,* 99).

Bonneville Baseball Park (*below*), between 800 and 900 South on Main and State Streets. The site is now occupied by Sears.

Saltair train. People would travel from downtown Salt Lake City by train and arrive at the resort, which lay at the end of a four thousand–foot causeway into the lake. "What forever separates my grandchildren from me is that they never had a glorious summer job at the age of fifteen, at Saltair, the stately pleasure dome that used to rise out of the waters of the Great Salt Lake, eighteen miles west of Salt Lake City. And they are never going to, for the Coney Island of the West is as dead as the dime hamburger, and all its folksy magic with it. It lasted sixty-five years, from 1893 to 1958, and then it died of change. I am one of the few remaining members of its cult, one of the last depositories of a fragment of its liturgy" ("Xanadu by the Salt Flats," 39).

Saltair, to the west of downtown on the south shore of the Great Salt Lake, ca. 1920s. The Saltair resort was built by the Church of Jesus Christ of Latter-day Saints and opened in June 1893. It burned down in 1925, was rebuilt in 1929, closed during World War II, and closed permanently in 1958. It later burned completely. "They [Stegner's grandchildren] know not the sound of gritty salt underfoot, or the sight of potted palms glittering with salt like tinsel. The smell of the humble hot dog cooking will never arouse them, as it does me, to uncontrollable glossolalia. Their ears will never prick, as mine do, to the spectral chanting of barkers, the thunder and screams from the roller coaster, the sob of saxophones from the dance floor. Nor will they ever hear, in intervals of quiet, the slap of heavy waves down under, down in the caverns measureless to man among the pilings" ("Xanadu by the Salt Flats," 39).

Salt Lake, Garfield, and Western Railroad passenger service to Saltair.

R. Owen Sweetman's Band, Saltair, ca. 1920s.

I&M Rug and Linoleum, 251 South State. The Irvine and Miller families owned the I&M Rug and Linoleum where Stegner worked after school as a clerk, salesman, and deliveryman. The business no longer exists.

The Brigham Street Pharmacy, South Temple (also known as Brigham Street) and E Street. The building no longer exists. When Bruce Mason "passes on the right, he looks for the Brigham Street Pharmacy, one hangout and landmark, universally known among the young as the BHP. It has become a shabby branch bank" (*Recapitulation,* 128).

Hotel Heron, 138 East 200 South, where George Stegner murdered Dorothy Webb LeRoy and killed himself on June 15, 1939. The building no longer exists. "Now he [Bruce Mason] looked east up First [*sic*] South, searching for the shabby Front, the dim apologetic sign, of the fleabag where he [Bo Mason] had killed himself. It, too, was gone" (*Recapitulation,* 83).

Hotel Utah Roof Garden, ca. 1920s. "In the old days
the Roof Garden had been open, with awnings and
pots and planters and the smell of freshly watered flowers. Now it was the Sky Room, enclosed for elegant
dining" (*Recapitulation*, 25).

Thomas Kearns mansion, 605 East South Temple, now
the Utah governor's mansion, April 1920. This, like the
David Keith mansion, is an example of the luxurious
homes built along South Temple from fortunes made
in Utah mining.

David Keith mansion, 529 East South Temple, 1920.

The Salt Lake Theatre, 100 South State Street, 1915, was one of the first theaters between Denver and the West Coast. It was built in 1861 and razed in 1928.

Temple Square Hotel, South Temple and West Temple Streets. "'Exactly Like You' means the carpet, the mezzanine, the very look and texture and smell, of the Temple Square Hotel" ("At Home in the Fields of the Lord,'" 166). The hotel also is the scene of Bruce Mason's seriocomic interlude with the elevator operator and Nola (*Recapitulation,* 66–71). It was demolished in January 2007 as a part of the downtown redevelopment.

Hotel Semloh, 107 East 200 South. The Green Dragon night club, where Bruce Mason would take a girl "to dance till the band folded" (*Recapitulation,* 51), was located inside.

Keith O'Brien Department Store, southwest corner,
300 South (Broadway) and State, June 1920. Later
became Auerbach's Department Store. This building
and its businesses were prominent landmarks in Salt
Lake City.

Utah Woolen Mills, 24–30 Richards Street, ca. 1920s. The business is still in existence, but at a new location at 59 West South Temple. Bruce Mason's varsity tennis letter sweater "might have come straight from its original Utah Woolen Mills box." The sweater was "a white cardigan with a red U above the pocket and four red stripes around the upper left sleeve" (*Recapitulation*, 151, 177).

Suicide Rock at the mouth of Parley's Canyon, looking west, 1907. This formation, now brightly decorated with signs and symbols painted by students, is still visible from Interstate 80 or Interstate 215 at the mouth of Parley's Canyon. The origin of the name is unknown.

Joe Hill.

Morrison Grocery, 778 South West Temple, where Joe Hill murdered grocer John Morrison and his son. This location is now an automobile dealership. Stegner tells the story of the murders and subsequent events in *Joe Hill,* a novel originally titled *The Preacher and the Slave.*

Utah State Penitentiary, located in what is now Sugar House Park, site of Joe Hill's execution in 1915. "I talked with the warden of the State Pen.... I got him to blindfold me and walk me through a mock execu-tion.... I got a criminal's-eye view of what it might feel [like] to be led out to your death" (Stegner and Etulain, *Conversations with Stegner*, 68).

Salt Lake City, looking northwest from 400 South between State Street and 200 East, May 1920.

Salt Lake City in the 1930s.

Main Street, looking north from
the Hotel Newhouse, June 1915.

Utah State Capitol and City Creek Canyon, July 1916.

Mount Olympus, as seen from West Jordan, April 1921, is a prominent peak in the southeast corner of the Salt Lake Valley. The rural expanse in the photo is now almost completely developed. Bruce Mason sees a storm gathering above the mountain as he waits in the Salt Lake City Cemetery (*Recapitulation,* 267).

Temple Square, August 1930. The sign and the arrow
pointing to the Salt Lake airport on the roof of the
Tabernacle were used by aviators.

Main Street, looking north from 300 South, 1930s.

West Temple and 200 South, looking east, 1918.

The Hotel Utah, April 22, 1919. This elegant hotel, located east of Temple Square, was for seventy-six years recognized as one of the most luxurious in the western United States. It is now the Joseph Smith Memorial Building.

Brooks Arcade Building, 268 South Main Street, May 1920. The building is representative of the downtown architecture of Salt Lake City in the early twentieth century.

Crowd watching the "Old Ironsides" electric score-
board at the Salt Lake Tribune Building on South Main
during a New York Yankees–St. Louis Cardinals World
Series game, October 7, 1928.

LDS Hospital, Eighth Avenue between C and
D Streets, 1912. Originally named the Dr. W. H.
Groves Latter-day Saint Hospital, it opened in 1905.

Holy Cross Hospital, 100 South between 1000 and
1100 East, 1905. Now the Salt Lake Regional Medical Center. The hospital was founded by the Catholic
Sisters of the Holy Cross in the late nineteenth century.

Brigham Young statue, Hotel Utah, city bus and streetcars on South Temple and Main Street. The statue was first displayed at Chicago's World Fair in 1893 and then moved temporarily to Temple Square and to the intersection of South Temple and Main Street. In 1993 it was moved to its present location a few feet to the north of the intersection directly west of the hotel.

Wagon train on South State Street, ca. 1920s.

Electric truck on South Temple near Temple Square, May 1918.

Truck and trailer on 200 North, May 1917. This picture shows what the Avenues and Federal Heights sections of Salt Lake looked like in the early twentieth century. Note the undeveloped road.

2100 South, looking east from State Street, January 1918. The Salt Lake County Hospital at the left no longer exists, and the site is now occupied by the Salt Lake County government complex.

Salt Lake City Brewing Company, 462 South 1000 East. As Chet Mason (Cecil Stegner) waits on Fourth South, he hears "the rumble of a truck coming down the unpaved hill past the old brewery ... the thud of a flat wheel on the street car as it came around the upper curve and started down around your corner" (*The Big Rock Candy Mountain*, 406).

Utah Light and Railway Company streetcar. "Something was missing and it took him nearly a block to realize what. Streetcars. Now it was buses rank with diesel exhaust and silent on rubber. Then it was yellow streetcars with square wheels, clanking, pounding, groaning on curves, audible for blocks (and welcome, too, for their shelter in the rain, warmth in the cold)" (*Recapitulation,* 74).

Pantages Theatre, 148 South Main, 1920. An example
of one of the many theaters located in downtown Salt
Lake City.

Auerbach's Department
Store, northeast corner of
State Street and 300 South,
later moved to the southwest
corner. Auerbach's was one of
the major department stores
in Salt Lake City.

Deseret News Building, southwest corner of Main Street and South Temple, 1912.

Sugar House, 1100 East 2100 South, panorama picture
taken from present location of Barnes and Noble Booksellers. Originally the site of a pioneer sugar refinery
and historically one of the prominent neighborhoods
in Salt Lake City, the area has largely maintained its
distinctive identity.

Devereaux House and Schramm-Johnson Drugstore, South Temple and 300 West, 1918. Originally built in 1857, the Devereaux House is now a reception center.

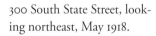

300 South State Street, looking northeast, May 1918.

Ruins of the Black Rock Resort on the south shore of
the Great Salt Lake, west of Saltair, September 1913.
Black Rock was a prominent resort area in the latter
half of the nineteenth century.

St. Mary's of the Wasatch College, 1928. The Catholic girls' school, near 1300 South, east of Foothill Village, closed in the early 1970s.

Brighton, ca. 1920s, where Elsa Mason goes to recuperate and Bruce is involved in a bitter scene with Jack Bailey and Nola Gordon (*Recapitulation,* 91, 215–33). Many people went to Brighton to escape the heat of Salt Lake City; it is now a ski resort.

Skating at Liberty Park, January 1917. Liberty Park is
one of Salt Lake City's two major parks. Stegner mentions it in both fiction and autobiography.

PART IV

⟶ *Maps* ⟵

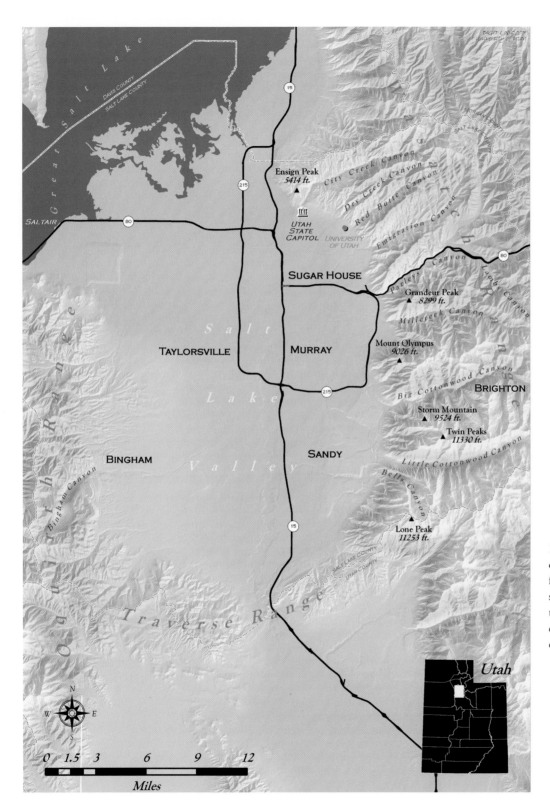

The Wasatch Front. This map covers an area of approximately forty-two by thirty miles and shows the three mountain ranges that ring the valley, the major canyons to the east, and the larger cities of the valley.

155

Salt Lake City. Salt Lake City has changed dramatically in the years since Stegner left the city. Not only are most of the older buildings gone or remodeled beyond recognition, but in the late 1960s Main Street was narrowed and the sidewalks were decorated with planters and stelae. In the late 1990s the Utah Transit Authority installed tracks on Main Street for the TRAX light-rail system, and in 2006 work began on the massive redevelopment of the two blocks between South Temple Street and 100 South Street and between West Temple Street and State Street.

Although the appearance of downtown Salt Lake City and the University of Utah has changed dramatically since Stegner left the city, the neighborhoods he knew—Sugar House, the lower Avenues, the areas south and east of the business district and near the university—have remained relatively unchanged. A walk through these areas would find them now much as Stegner knew them in the 1920s and 1930s.

Named sites in *italics* are no longer standing.

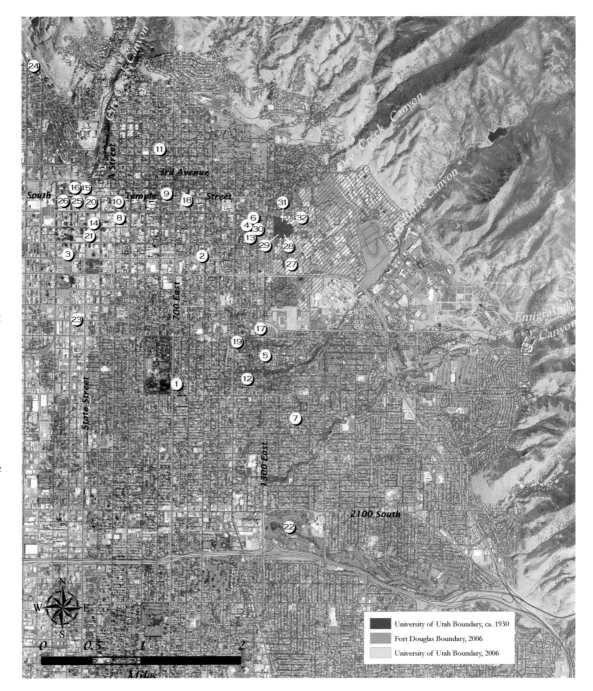

STEGNER ADDRESSES IN SALT LAKE CITY

Because they moved so frequently, the Stegners were not always listed in the city directory.

1. 1191 South 700 East (1922, the Stegner family)

2. *873 East 400 South* (1925, the Stegner family)

3. *26 West 400 South* (1926, the Stegner family)

4. 1155 East 200 South (1927, Wallace)

5. 1008 South 1300 East (year uncertain, but Wallace is known to have lived one year with the Robert Irvine family while attending the university)

6. 148 East 700 South (1929, George, Hilda, and Wallace)

7. 1440 South 1500 East (1930–1931, George, Hilda, and Wallace)

8. 125 South 300 East (1934, George)

9. 621 South Temple (1934, George)

10. 53 South 300 East (1935, George)

11. 280 G Street (1935, Wallace and Mary)

12. 1211 East Princeton (1936, Wallace and Mary)

13. 270 South 1200 East (1937, Wallace and Mary)

PLACES MENTIONED IN STEGNER'S WORKS OR RELATED TO STEGNER'S LIFE

14. *Hotel Heron,* 138 East 200 South

15. Hotel Utah, 15 East South Temple (later and currently the Joseph Smith Memorial Building). The Brigham Young Monument was first displayed at the Chicago's World Fair in 1893 and then moved temporarily to Temple Square and to the intersection of South Temple and Main Street in 1997. In 1993 it was moved to its present location a few feet to the north.

16. *Temple Square Hotel,* 71 West South Temple (redevelopment has eliminated this site)

17. East High School, 1300 East 900 South (a new building is located on the site of the building where Stegner attended school)

18. *Morrison Grocery,* 778 South West Temple (the site of the murders of grocer John G. Morrison and his son John Arling Morrison, for which Joe Hill was executed by firing squad at the state prison in Sugar House on November 19, 1915)

19. *Salt Lake Tennis Club,* 245 South 1100 East (now the Tenth East Senior Center)

20. Salt Lake Public Library, 15 South State Street (later the Hansen Planetarium and presently vacant)

21. I&M Rug and Linoleum, 251 South State Street (business no longer in existence)

22. *Utah State Prison* (now Sugar House Park)

23. *Bonneville Baseball Park,* 800 South between Main and State Streets; the site is now occupied by Sears)

24. Warm Springs, 840 North 300 West (business no longer in existence; building presently vacant)

25. *ZCMI,* 15 South Main Street (redevelopment has eliminated this site)

26. Utah Woolen Mills, 24–30 Richards Street (business still in existence at new location, 59 West South Temple)

UNIVERSITY OF UTAH SITES

27. *Cummings Field/Ute Stadium* (site now occupied by Rice-Eccles Stadium)

28. John R. Park Building

29. George Thomas Library (later the Utah Museum of Natural History)

30. Sigma Nu, 200 South between 1200 East and 1300 East

31. Kingsbury Hall

32. LeRoy Cowles Building (location of the English Department in Stegner's time; currently used by the Mathematics Department)

Notes

CROSSROADS OF THE WEST

1. For the history of Salt Lake City and its valley, one should consult Thomas G. Alexander, *Utah, the Right Place: The Official Centennial History;* Will Bagley, ed., *The Pioneer Camp of the Saints: The 1846 and 1847 Mormon Trail Journals of Thomas Bullock;* Peter H. DeLafosse, ed., *Trailing the Pioneers: A Guide to Utah's Emigrant Trails, 1829–1869;* John S. McCormick, *Salt Lake City: The Gathering Place;* Dale L. Morgan, *The Great Salt Lake;* Linda Sillitoe, *A History of Salt Lake County;* and Gary Topping, ed., *Great Salt Lake: An Anthology.*

2. Bagley, *Pioneer Camp of the Saints,* 235.

3. Roberts, *A Comprehensive History of the Church of Jesus Christ of Latter-day Saints: Century I,* 1:311.

4. Stegner, "Finding the Place," 18, 15–16.

5. Sillitoe, *History of Salt Lake County,* 105–6.

6. Stegner, "Fields of the Lord," in *The Sound of Mountain Water: The Changing American West,* 163; in *Marking the Sparrow's Fall: Wallace Stegner's American West,* 33.

7. Stegner, *Recapitulation,* 3.

8. Ibid., 4.

9. Ibid., 21.

10. Stegner, *The Big Rock Candy Mountain,* 374.

11. Ibid.

12. Stegner, "Fields of the Lord," in *Sound of Mountain Water,* 166; in *Marking the Sparrow's Fall,* 35.

13. "Love of Books," 111.

14. Stegner, "Xanadu by the Salt Flats," 39, 45.

SALT LAKE CITY

1. Stegner, "Finding the Place," 17–18.

2. Stegner, "Fields of the Lord," in *Sound of Mountain Water,* 157; in *Marking the Sparrow's Fall,* 29.

3. Ibid., 158.

4. Ibid., 158–59.

5. Stegner, "Finding the Place," 12–13.

6. Stegner and Etulain, *Conversations with Wallace Stegner on Western History and Literature,* 13.

7. Stegner, "Letter, Much Too Late," 29.

8. Ibid., 24.

9. Hepworth, "Wallace Stegner," 25–26.

10. Stegner, "Born a Square," 171.

11. Stegner, "The Last of the Exterminators," in *Wolf Willow,* 73–74.

12. Stegner, "Coda: Wilderness Letter," 153.

13. Stegner, *A Shooting Star,* 384–85; Stegner, "Born a Square," 180.

14. Stegner, *Recapitulation,* 242, 269.

15. Benson, *Wallace Stegner: His Life and Work,* 384–85.

16. Stegner and Etulain, *Conversations with Stegner,* 42.

17. Benson, *Wallace Stegner,* 4.

EAST HIGH SCHOOL

1. Stegner, *Big Rock Candy Mountain,* 400–403.

2. Stegner and Etulain, *Conversations with Stegner,* 11.

3. Stegner, "Finding the Place," 16–17.

4. Stegner, *Recapitulation,* 31.

5. Stegner, "The Volunteer," in *Collected Stories of Wallace Stegner,* 292.

6. Ibid., 296–309; Stegner, *Recapitulation,* 37–48.

7. Stegner, *Recapitulation,* 19.

8. Stegner, *Big Rock Candy Mountain,* 376.

9. *CMTC: Fort Douglas, 1938,* n.p., 2 (quote), 3.

10. Stegner, *Recapitulation,* 92–93.

11. Stegner, "Fields of the Lord," in *Sound of Mountain Water,* 167; in *Marking the Sparrow's Fall,* 36.

THE UNIVERSITY OF UTAH

1. Angleman, "Gone the Meadowlarks," 171.

2. Ralph V. Chamberlin, *The University of Utah: A History of Its First Hundred Years, 1850 to 1950,* 392, 424.

3. Ibid., 371–73.

4. Angleman, "Gone the Meadowlarks," 72.

5. Chamberlin, *University of Utah,* 447.

6. 1927 *Utonian,* 351, 352.

7. 1931 *Utonian,* 359, 357.

8. Chamberlin, *University of Utah,* 435.

9. Stegner, "Love of Books," 120.

10. *Time,* June 18, 1965, 74–78; July 19, 1964, 50–51.

11. McCormick, *Salt Lake City,* 146.

12. Stegner's spellings of his friends' names in "It Is the Love of Books I Owe Them" are occasionally wrong. The correct spellings are given here.

13. Stegner, "Finding the Place," 17.

14. Stegner, "Love of Books," 116.

15. 1931 *Utonian,* 231.

16. Stegner, *Recapitulation,* 107–9.

17. Ibid., 128, 132.

18. Ibid., 5.

19. Ibid., 62–64, 65.

20. Ibid., 155.

21. Ibid., 160.

22. Stegner and Etulain, *Conversations with Stegner,* 8; Hepworth, *Stealing Glances,* 87.

23. Stegner, "Love of Books," 120.

Bibliography

Alexander, Thomas G. *Utah, the Right Place: The Official Centennial History.* Salt Lake City: Gibbs Smith, 1995.

Angleman, Sydney W. "Gone the Meadowlarks." In *Remembering,* edited by Elizabeth Haglund, 69–82. Salt Lake City: University of Utah Press, 1981.

Bagley, Will, ed. *The Pioneer Camp of the Saints: The 1846 and 1847 Mormon Trail Journals of Thomas Bullock.* Spokane: Arthur H. Clark, 2001.

Benson, Jackson J. *Wallace Stegner: His Life and Work.* New York: Viking, 1996.

Chamberlin, Ralph V. *The University of Utah: A History of Its First Hundred Years, 1850 to 1950.* Edited by Harold W. Bentley. Salt Lake City: University of Utah Press, 1960.

CMTC: Fort Douglas, 1938. Salt Lake City: Stevens and Wallis, 1938.

Colberg, Nancy. *Wallace Stegner: A Descriptive Bibliography.* Lewiston, Idaho: Confluence Press, 1990.

DeLafosse, Peter H., ed. *Trailing the Pioneers: A Guide to Utah's Emigrant Trails, 1829–1869.* Logan: Utah State University Press, 1994.

Hepworth, James R. *Stealing Glances: Three Interviews with Wallace Stegner.* Albuquerque: University of New Mexico Press, 1998.

———. "Wallace Stegner: The Quiet Revolutionary." In *Wallace Stegner: Man and Writer,* edited by Charles E. Rankin, 17–26. Albuquerque: University of New Mexico Press, 1997.

McCormick, John S. *Salt Lake City: The Gathering Place.* Woodland Hills, Calif.: Windsor Publications, 1980.

Morgan, Dale L. *The Great Salt Lake.* Indianapolis: Bobbs-Merrill, 1947.

Roberts, B. H. *A Comprehensive History of the Church of Jesus Christ of Latter-day Saints: Century I.* 6 vols. Salt Lake City: Deseret News Press, 1930.

Robinson, Forrest G., and Margaret G. Robinson. *Wallace Stegner.* Twayne United States Authors Series. Boston: Twayne Publishers, 1977.

Scholl, Barry, and Francois Camoin. *Utah, a Guide to the State: Revised Travel Guide.* Salt Lake City: Gibbs Smith, 1998.

Sillitoe, Linda. *A History of Salt Lake County.* Utah Centennial County History Series. Salt Lake City: Utah State Historical Society, 1996.

Stegner, Wallace. "At Home in the Fields of the Lord." In *The Sound of Mountain Water: The Changing American West,* 157–69. New York: Doubleday, 1997. First published as "Hometown Revisited: 15. Salt Lake City." *Tomorrow* 9 (February 1950): 26–29. Reprinted in *Marking the Sparrow's Fall: Wallace Stegner's American West,* 29–37. New York: Henry Holt, 1998.

———. *The Big Rock Candy Mountain.* New York: Penguin, 1991. First published by Doubleday, 1943.

———. "Born a Square." In *The Sound of Mountain Water: The Changing American West,* 170–85. New York: Penguin, 1997. First published in *Atlantic* 213 (January 1964): 46–50. Reprinted in *The Sound of Mountain Water: The Changing American West,* 170–85. New York: Henry Holt, 1969.

———. "Coda: Wilderness Letter." In *The Sound of Mountain Water: The Changing American West,* 147–53. New York: Penguin, 1997.

———. *Collected Stories of Wallace Stegner.* New York: Penguin, 1991. First published by Random House, 1990.

————. "Finding the Place: A Migrant Childhood." In *Where the Bluebird Sings to the Lemonade Springs: Living and Writing in the West,* 3–21. New York: Random House, 1992. Also published in *Growing Up Western,* edited by Clarus Backes, 153–85. New York: Alfred A. Knopf, 1989.

————. "It Is the Love of Books I Owe Them." In *Remembering,* edited by Elizabeth Haglund, 111–20. Salt Lake City: University of Utah Press, 1981.

————. *Joe Hill: A Biographical Novel.* New York: Penguin, 1990. First published as *The Preacher and the Slave.* Garden City, N.Y.: Doubleday, 1950.

————. "Letter, Much Too Late." In *Where the Bluebird Sings to the Lemonade Springs: Living and Writing in the West,* 22–33. New York: Random House, 1992.

————. *Recapitulation.* New York: Penguin, 1997. First published by Doubleday, 1979.

————. *A Shooting Star.* New York: Penguin, 1996. First published by Viking, 1961.

————. *The Sound of Mountain Water.* New York: Doubleday, 1997.

————. *Where the Bluebird Sings to the Lemonade Springs: Living and Writing in the West.* New York: Random House, 1992.

————. *Wolf Willow: A History, a Story, and a Memory of the Last Plains Frontier.* New York: Penguin, 1990. First published by Viking, 1962.

————. "Xanadu by the Salt Flats: Memories of a Pleasure Dome." In *Marking the Sparrow's Fall: Wallace Stegner's American West,* edited by Page Stegner, 38–45. New York: Henry Holt, 1998. First published in *American Heritage* (June–July 1981): 81–89.

Stegner, Wallace, and Richard W. Etulain. *Conversations with Wallace Stegner on Western History and Literature.* Foreword by Norman Cousins. Rev. ed. Salt Lake City: University of Utah Press, 1990.

Topping, Gary, ed. *Great Salt Lake: An Anthology.* Logan: Utah State University Press, 2002.

University of Utah catalogs, 1925–1931 and 1934–1937.

The Utonian. University of Utah student yearbooks for 1925–1931 and 1934–1937.